MORE
BOYS & GIRLS
OF HISTORY

Linlithgow Castle (Birthplace of Mary Queen of Scots)

MORE
BOYS & GIRLS
OF HISTORY

BY

RHODA & EILEEN POWER

CAMBRIDGE

At the University Press

1953

CAMBRIDGE UNIVERSITY PRESS
Cambridge, New York, Melbourne, Madrid, Cape Town,
Singapore, São Paulo, Delhi, Tokyo, Mexico City

Cambridge University Press
The Edinburgh Building, Cambridge CB2 8RU, UK

Published in the United States of America by Cambridge University Press, New York

www.cambridge.org
Information on this title: www.cambridge.org/9780521236041

First published 1928
Reprinted 1936
"   1942
"   1945
"   1953
First paperback edition 2011

A catalogue record for this publication is available from the British Library

ISBN 978-0-521-23604-1 Paperback

To
GERALDINE CLEGG

PREFACE

THE kind welcome which our first volume, *Boys and Girls of History*, received both from boys and girls and from their parents and teachers has encouraged us to tell the stories of some more children. This time we have tried in the main to illustrate the history of discovery and the growth of "Greater Britain," and our stories all belong to the period subsequent to the middle ages. If they can claim any originality, it lies in the fact that we have tried to see the events described not only through the eyes of the adventuring or conquering English, but through those of the little Irish girl, the Red Indian princess, or the chief's son of Kandy, the Burmese, the Maori and the Australian "Blackfellow," and have attempted to describe their daily lives. We have shown splendid failure as well as splendid success, the desertion of Henry Hudson by his sailors and the execution of Ralegh, as well as the triumphant return of Cabot and the growth of the East India Company. But as every boy and girl likes adventure, and the boys and girls in these stories witnessed or shared in a stirring adventure, the history of England overseas, we hope that this book will be as fortunate in winning their approval as the first.

R. D. P.
E. E. P.

October 1928

CONTENTS

NOTE

The end-paper map has been specially drawn
for this book by Elinor Lambert.

The illustration on p. 139 is from a block supplied by Messrs John Lane; that on p. 243 is
reproduced by permission of Messrs Routledge;
those on pp. 259 and 269 by arrangement with
Messrs Sampson Low and Marston.

ILLUSTRATIONS

CHAPTER I

THE BRISTOL APPRENTICE

[A.D. 1497. Cabot discovers Newfoundland]

The church was almost in darkness, but the dim light from two candles on the altar flickered against the small, perfect model of a ship, making it seem to move as though it were rocking on invisible waves. With bowed head the priest stood, intoning the Latin prayers, and one behind the other knelt the twelve poor sailors, maintained by the Fraternity of Mariners to pray for all merchants and seamen labouring on the water. Their hoods had fallen back from their grey heads and their brown weather-beaten faces were grave. Ned saw them as he pushed open the door and a long dusty ray of light brought a gleam of sunshine into the building.

The boy pulled off his flat woollen cap and knelt behind the sailors, peering round a pillar so as to see the little ship, which grateful citizens had placed in the church as a symbol that it had pleased God to send wealth and glory to Bristol from the sea. The cold from the stone floor penetrated Ned's coarse frieze hose, and although it was summer he shivered under his blue coat whenever the door creaked and a fresh draught of air dispersed the smell of incense and showed that some new passer-by had come in to pray.

There were women in the church, now. Ned's eyes had grown accustomed to the darkness and he could see them kneeling in a little group under a stained glass window, which cast its colours on their pale faces and on the white linen partlets at their necks. Their heads bowed rhythmically to the droning voice of the priest and whenever they heard the word *Matthew* they crossed themselves, and their eyes opened, looking towards the little ship. Ned knew them. They came into church every day to pray for their husbands and sons, who had sailed away on the *Matthew* three long months ago, and had not yet returned.

Whispering a prayer of his own, the boy muttered "Amen," rose quietly to his feet and leaned against a pillar. Gazing wistfully at the little model, he thought of the *Matthew* and her master, John Cabot the Venetian. Even the city apprentices knew Cabot for a dreamer of dreams, who listened to the tales of every fisherman mending his nets on the shore, and every mariner sunning his weather-beaten face on the Bristol sands. And now he had gone with a patent from King Henry VII to "seek, subdue and occupy" any region unknown to Christians, to set up a royal banner and possess these lands as the King's vassal. He had gone, the dreamer, with a ship that was smaller than the best merchant vessels and a crew of sixteen.

Sebastian Cabot
(*Son of John Cabot*)

Ned had a brother called Tom on the *Matthew*. He sighed as he thought of him, trying to choke the feelings of envy which rose in his heart. Standing in the cool, dark church, with the smell of incense in his nostrils and the murmur of prayers around him, he could almost see the *Matthew* as she lay at anchor on that May morning with the little fishing-boats rocking beside her, the clumsy cogs pushing out of the harbour and a beautiful merchant ship, square rigged, with a castle fore and aft, sweeping round the bend with the sun on her sails.

There was a crowd on the shore that day. Apprentices, blue-coated like himself, pushed their way towards the front, shouting insults and ducking when the citizens cuffed them for their "mannerless japes." The city sheriffs had come to keep order and a few merchants were standing in clusters. Ned admired their velvet caps and their coloured tunics and hose which were half-hidden by those new loose gowns with the full hanging sleeves. They were talking together, some saying " 'Tis a fool's quest," others stroking their chins and murmuring doubtfully, "We have adventured such cheap merchandise as caps and small knives." Bristol seamen who had trafficked in Ireland and Iceland argued eagerly, telling the time-worn tale of an island which Irish fishermen had seen in the far west and called the Isle of the Blest. They chattered and laughed, half credulous, half mocking, speaking of the Icelanders and their stories of a shadowy coast to which their ancestors had sailed. Ned remembered how the women had stood beside them, interrupting and teasing; the poor ones in the usual coarse gowns and old-fashioned wimples which hid their throats, the rich merchants' wives in handsome flowing dresses clasped with jewelled belts and cut square at the neck to show their golden chains. He could still see how the wind fluttered the white kerchiefs on their heads and made their coloured veils float out behind until they caught and held them. He could see himself, too, a sturdy, muscular lad of eleven, in charge of his master's daughter. He was carrying her on his back and she clasped her little hands round his neck and rubbed her cheek against his head saying, "Never mind, Ned, never mind." He had turned a grateful face towards her and given her an affectionate squeeze for he knew what she meant.

The night before the *Matthew* had sailed he had tried to board her and with the help of his brother Tom had hidden behind some barrels as a stowaway, but the cooper had found him and had ducked him in the dirty harbour water till, gasping and spluttering, he had howled for mercy, only to be kicked ashore where he grazed his nose on the pebbles. With his eyes smarting from the salt water and his nose bleeding down his blue tunic, he had slunk home, soaking wet, and had startled his master's family by appearing in the doorway blubbering, "I don't want to be a shoemaker! I want to go to sea!" and dripping all over the clean rushes. He had expected rough treatment for running away, but instead they had made him peel off his wet clothes and sit, rolled in a blanket, in front of the kitchen fire, drinking a hot posset. Everyone had been very kind and the master's wife, after scolding him gently for spoiling his new outfit, had washed his nose and put a plaster on it. Little Mistress Peg, crying, "Poor 'prentice hurted!" had, to Ned's horror, run into the shop to fetch her father and of course the master had come in. He pretended to be in a great pother, but he pulled Ned's hair saying "What's this? My new apprentice comes home half-drowned and then wants to go to sea. Well, well, well! A pretty piece of work you've given St Crispin to-day, sirrah." At this Ned had laughed, for he knew that St Crispin was the patron saint who watched over shoemakers, and so the matter had dropped. Nevertheless, tears were very near to his eyes when he stood on the quay and watched the *Matthew* sailing away, with Master John Cabot standing on the quarter-deck and waving his velvet hat.

The picture had come so vividly before him that Ned rubbed his eyes and, looking a little dazed, stole tip-toe through the church door and into the sunny close. He pushed past the beggars who sat with outstretched hands at the porch, showing their sores and crippled limbs, and he looked up and down the street, trying to remember the house at which he was to leave the new scarlet slippers hanging on a cord over his arm. His visit to the church had brought peace to his mind and, although he still had a slight twinge of envy when he thought of Tom, he felt that if he could not go to sea on a voyage of discovery, he was doing the next best thing by living in one of the busiest of English sea-ports, where tales of adventure were as full of flavour as the dried prunes which the Venetians brought to England in their galleys.

He paused for a minute and gazed about him. Bristol certainly looked prosperous. The little shops, open to the street, were doing brisk trade. He could see the apprentices and journeymen sitting at the back, toiling busily. Sometimes a master-craftsman left his shop and strode from house to house, inspecting the work of his fellow-gildsmen, and carrying out his duties as a warden of the trade. Dogs nosed among the heaps of garbage at the street corners and from the smaller alleys came the cries "Whiting, maids, whiting!" "Hot pies!" "Fine brooms to sell! Green brooms, new broo-oo-ooms!" where the street-sellers sauntered up and down, tapping at doors and gazing into windows. Here and there an elderly serving-maid was haggling over a purchase, and a young one, giggling and blushing, was paying too much for a worthless article because she had been told that her face was her fortune. Cripples with their knees and hands protected by wooden blocks crawled along the cobbles whining for alms, and sometimes a cart laden with fish clattered past while the driver cried, "Make way," and ladies with sensitive nostrils wrinkled their noses delicately, stooping under the counters into the shops or pressing back against the walls to avoid the wheels.

Ned kept to the better streets and after delivering his slippers at a fine, three-storied mansion, strolled homewards. He loved to see the merchants' beautiful timbered dwellings towering above the little shops with their swinging signs and overhanging penthouses. And, as he passed, he nodded to himself, thinking that if he could not go to sea, he would be a merchant and have a ship of his own, like the rich traders of Bristol, or perhaps share a fleet with several others not quite so wealthy or well known as himself. He would build himself just such a house as every successful merchant loved to have, a house with several rooms and a dining-hall where musicians would play from a gallery hung with tapestries. There should be vaults underground where the goods could be stored. He had been in such vaults and had

A Street in old Bristol

(*The illustration shows Bristol as it was at the beginning of the nineteenth century*)

laughed to think that he was under the street
and somebody else's shop. If he were very
rich and had not space enough in his own
cellars, he would hire another or have a tene-
ment in a different part of the town like other
merchants, and here he would sit in a counting-
house and check the goods and the money, and
soon become so rich that he would entertain the
royal family just as the merchants had done last
year when King Henry VII had visited Bristol.

His reverie was interrupted by a titter behind
him, and a voice wailing, "I don't want t-to be
a shoemaker. I w-want to go to sea. Boo hoo!"
Somebody pulled off his cap and shouted "*Stow-
away!*" and before he knew where he was half-
a-dozen bakers' apprentices were dancing round
him shouting, "He wants to go to sea! Boo
hoo! He wants to go to sea." Ned laid about
him lustily, shouting, "Shoemakers to the
rescue! Clubs, Clubs!"

Being at the corner of Shoe Lane, he had no
trouble in attracting attention. In the twinkling
of an eye the boys of his own trade were on the
scene, belabouring the young bakers with their
clubs, their fists, their feet, until the whole street
was in an uproar. Women, grasping their children, fled for safety. Dogs barked and tripped
up the youngsters, who did not even stop fighting while they were sprawling on the ground.
An old gentleman, grumbling, "Those rascally
apprentices," laid about him with a stick which

a clubless boy seized and turned to greater advantage, while a beggar with a bandage over one eye waved a crutch in the air, crying hoarsely "England for ever!" until a sheriff appeared round the corner, when he hastily adjusted his bandage and hobbled up the street, whining, "Have pity on the blind. For the mercy of heaven spare the poor blind man a coin."

In the midst of the turmoil all the church bells began suddenly to ring and a man on horseback came galloping up the street shouting, "The *Matthew's* come home!"

The fight stopped like magic. Swift as the wind each apprentice raced towards the harbour. Heads popped out of windows, craftsmen left their tools and ran, while the fat old sheriff waddled in the rear, trying to look dignified but puffing breathlessly with excitement.

Down by the water stood a crowd of women and children laughing, crying and blowing kisses. Tough old salts, who had not handled an oar for many a day, were rowing anyone who would pay to get a closer view of the ship, for there lay the *Matthew* with all her pennons flying and Master John Cabot climbing down a rope-ladder into the boat below.

Screaming "Tom! Tom! Tom!" Ned sped along the quay, only stopping when a fisherman seized him to prevent him from leaping into the water.

A forest of hands stretched out to help Cabot

ashore and from lip to lip passed the wonderful message, "He's found a new island!" Then came his seamen, caught and hugged by their wives and mothers till they scarcely had breath to tell of the unknown coast, where the cod were so plentiful that men could catch them in baskets. Somebody muttered, "We've cod enough! Where are the gold and spices of Asia?" But nobody took any notice. Men, women and children could do nothing but clamour for the story, calling to one another, "He's discovered a new isle!"

When Ned had found Tom, he sat on a piece of driftwood, listening so long to the tale that he did not reach home until it was dark and the shutters were closed and the door bolted. He knocked with his club, but excitement seemed to have muddled his mind for he could not even answer a plain question.

"Where have you been?" asked the shoe-maker.

"He's found a new isle!" answered Ned.

Luckily the information was so welcome that Ned was not even scolded, and he went to bed dreaming that he had sailed to the west in an enormous shoe, and had found Cabot as a stow-away.

It was four days later that he had the proudest moment of his life. He was alone in the shop. The master was away and the journeyman out

on some errand. The apprentice was stitching
at his leather when he was disturbed by the
sound of voices. He jumped up and leaned
across the counter, and there was Cabot coming
up the street, surrounded by young men, all
urging him to talk, crying, "Take me, too,
sir." "My father's a mariner, 'tis in the blood."
And Cabot was testily pushing them aside,
saying, "Out of my way, young men, and let
me purchase my clothes in peace."

Ned knew that the King had given him ten
pounds as a reward for finding the island, and
he wondered how much he had left, for he
looked very grand in his new doublet and
jewelled hat. But his shoes were torn.

Ned's heart leaped. He blushed, stammered
for a minute, then boldly cried, "What lack ye?
What lack ye? Here's fine leather for shoes,
scarlet, green and black. What do ye lack?"

To his joy and amazement Cabot swung
through the little aperture in the counter,
walked into the shop and sat on the cobbler's
bench with his right foot stretched out.

That evening Ned sauntered through Bread
Street. "Boo hoo! Stowaway!" grinned the
young apprentices.

Ned tossed his head. "Yah!" he sneered.
"Who's jealous?"

After all, a baker's boy could never measure
Cabot for a pair of shoes.

CHAPTER II

THE CHILDHOOD OF MARY QUEEN OF SCOTS

[A.D. 1542–1558]

"By this post one came to the King out of Linlithgow, showing to him good tidings that the Queen was delivered. The King enquired whether it was a man-child or a woman. The messenger said: 'It is a fair daughter.' The King answered: 'Adieu, farewell. It [the Kingdom of Scotland] came with a lass and it will pass with a lass.' And so he recommended himself to the mercy of Almighty God and spake little from that time forth, but turned his back unto his lords and his face unto the wall.... In this manner he departed...and yielded his spirit to God."

It was Sunday, September 9, 1543. Soldiers guarded the gates of Stirling Castle. Men and women in gala robes, children perching on their fathers' shoulders and citizens of every trade and profession stood outside, eagerly staring up at the windows, while the young apprentices, who had a holiday, were pushing their way to the front of the crowd, longing for a glimpse of the baby Queen Mary.

The child, who was barely nine months old, was being crowned in the Chapel Royal and the castle was gay with banners and flowers. Within the chapel stood cardinal and bishop, lord and lady. Scarlet robes and embroidered vestments glowed softly in the candle-light. Jewels sparkled. Silks and satins glittered with precious stones and, as the choristers passed swinging censers on silver chains, the heavy scent of incense hung in the air. The baby, wrapped in brocade and lace, sat in her mother's arms, attended by her nurse and the ladies of her court. With wide solemn eyes she stared at the brilliant throng, but when the crown was placed on her forehead, her tiny hand raised to the

Stirling Castle

sceptre and the Scottish lords in their tartans knelt before her, paying homage, her brow puckered and above the low murmuring of the oath of allegiance her voice rose in a thin querulous wail. The ladies turned towards her and those who were superstitious crossed themselves. Outside, among the waiting crowds, somebody whispered "The babe wept," and people looked at one another in consternation, muttering "An evil omen! The reign has begun with tears."

Tears and trouble followed for many a year, but the little Queen was at first too young to understand. She did not know that the English King, Henry VIII, had already sought her in marriage for his son, hoping that he might become her guardian and in this way control the Kingdom of Scotland. She did not know that because his demands were resisted, he had threatened to steal her and had sent his soldiers to invade her country. She only knew that she had often to make long journeys from one castle to another, sometimes sitting in a heavy covered carriage on the knees of her nurse, Janet Sinclair, with the four Marys, her maids of honour, beside her and a strong guard of soldiers all round; sometimes riding in the arms of a Scottish lord, with a cavalcade of ladies and gentlemen in front and behind and guards armed with pikes and muskets on each side.

Unconscious of the fighting on the border and of the blood which was being shed on her account, the little Queen spent happy days in her tapestried nurseries, playing at ball and ninepins, dressing her wooden dolls in silk and velvet robes with peaked bodices and long full skirts like her own, and covering their painted hair with white lawn coifs.

With the exception of her frequent journeys, Mary led a quiet childish life until she was five years old. Then, one day, when she was playing in her nursery at Stirling Castle, her mother sent for her. With her brown hair drawn tightly back under a cap sewn with pearls, Mary, in a heavy grown-up gown with long stiff sleeves, went down the narrow winding staircase into a room where the stone walls were hung with tapestries and paintings and the floor was strewn with rushes. Here, leaning against her mother's shoulder, she was told that she was going to be married.

Young as she was, Mary understood, for she had often played at weddings with her dolls, and she probably asked many questions about the bridegroom, although her mother could only tell her that he was the eldest son of the French King, a small fair-haired delicate boy, called Francis, who was not yet five years old.

The little Queen's mother was a French-woman, Mary of Guise, and the child had heard many a tale of France from her lips and could prattle in French, too, so that she was excited when she learned that in a few months she would sail across the sea to her mother's country and meet her bridegroom.

Preparations for her departure now began to disturb Mary's quiet life, and many a time she was called from the castle garden and interrupted in her games, to stand before a mirror while dressmakers and tailors littered her room with silks and velvets and rich brocades, or spread before her cloth of gold and silver tissue. There followed such a measuring, cutting and pinning that the child must have grown weary of her trousseau before she had met her bridegroom. Nevertheless, it was a gay little maiden who set sail in August 1548, accompanied by a fleet of French ships and a retinue which included her own four Marys and her nurse, a governess and two hundred gentlemen and servants.

The weather was bad, but Mary must have enjoyed the voyage, for one of the French lords who had charge of her wrote to her mother, saying "The Queen your daughter...prospers and is as full of good cheer as ever you saw her. She has been less ill upon the sea than anyone of her company, so that she made fun of those that were."

Mary's arrival caused her escort great anxiety, for she landed at Roscoff in Brittany, on one of the most perilous coasts in Europe. As the pilot guided her galley into the harbour, waves were breaking over the half-sunken reefs and swift currents were running between the islands. Breton fishermen in boats with orange sails cheered the ships as, one after another, they put to shore, but there was great disappointment in

Roscoff when the little Queen left after two nights and continued her journey.

Apartments had been arranged for her in a Dominican convent at Morlaix, and the Lord of Rohan, a Breton noble, and his suite rode to meet her, conducting her with great ceremony to her rooms. To most small children, the strange faces and costumes, the crowds, the pomp and all the discomforts of a long journey would have been alarming, but neither Mary's health nor her spirits seemed to suffer, and she enjoyed herself far more than the escort responsible for her welfare. At Morlaix, that escort had at least one moment of anxiety which was nothing but an adventure in the eyes of the little Queen. Mary had been to the church with her governess, her own retinue and the Breton nobles, to sing the *Te Deum* and give thanks for her safe arrival. She returned to the town in a litter, crossed the drawbridge and passed through the city gates, when there was a crash and a loud cry behind her. The drawbridge, overburdened with horsemen, broke so that many of the Queen's gentlemen fell into the river. Seeing their plight, those Scottish nobles who had remained in the town drew their swords and shouting "Treason, treason!" tried to surround Mary and protect her. But the Lord of Rohan was walking by the little girl's litter. Throwing back his head, he cried in ringing tones which were heard above the tumult: "No Breton was ever a traitor." He proved his words, for during the two days on which Mary was at Morlaix, he had all the gates of the town taken off their hinges and the chains of the bridges broken. Any traitor could have come into the city and injured the Queen, but the Bretons had proud hospitable natures. If they had disliked her, they would have been ashamed to harm her, for she had been entrusted to their care. But they loved her. In two days, "this little lady," as they called her, had won their hearts, and a man who had seen her wrote:

The young Queen was at that time one of the most perfect creatures that the God of Nature ever formed, for that her equal was nowhere to be found, nor had the world another child of her fortune and hope.

Indeed, Mary captivated everyone with her charming manners and her quaint grown-up graces. One of her admirers called her "a little rosebud." Another described her as "the best and prettiest young queen that can be in the world" and even her stern old grandmother, Antoinette de Bourbon, who came to meet her and take her to the court, wrote:

She is very pretty indeed, and as intelligent a child as you could see. Her hair is dark and her complexion clear. I think that when she develops she will be a beautiful girl, for her complexion is fine and her skin

Mary Queen of Scots
(*at the age of nine*)

white. The lower part of the face is very well formed, the eyes are small and rather deep set, the face is somewhat long. She is graceful and self-assured. To sum up, we may be well pleased with her.

The little Dauphin, her future husband, was just as pleased with Mary as his elders, and when she arrived at the court in St Germain en Laye he soon made friends with her and was never so happy as when he was playing with her. The children's friendship delighted the French King, Henry II, who was determined that Mary should be brought up with his own sons and daughters, until she and the Dauphin were old enough to be married. He made special arrangements for her comfort, ordering the castle to be thoroughly cleaned before she arrived and forbidding any workman or stranger to enter the city if he had come from a place where there was an infectious disease. He not only looked after her welfare, but he commanded all the towns through which she passed to receive and honour her in a manner suited to a queen, and he even gave her the power to grant pardons and set prisoners free.

In the royal nursery at St Germain, the little girl began her education. At first she kept her own nurse and her Scottish governess, but after a while French ladies and tutors were added to her suite and many of her Scottish attendants went home.

After the Dauphin, her greatest friend was Madame Ysabel, or Elizabeth of Valois, the French King's eldest daughter. She was younger than Mary, but the two children had lessons together. They learned how to read and write and how to embroider in wool and silk. They studied French literature and foreign languages and they made verses. Sometimes, instead of writing essays, they sent one another letters in Latin on some subject which their tutors had set. They were taught music, singing and dancing, and they spent many an hour practising on the harp. Since both were destined for royal bridegrooms, they had to learn all the accomplishments that the French court could teach them.

Although their tutors and governesses kept them busily employed, the royal children did not spend all their time at work. The French court was gay and the little people were just as fond of amusement as their elders. They delighted in games and had many companions who shared their play, for thirty-seven children from noble families were brought up with the Dauphin and his brothers. Mary, of course, joined in all the fun, but because she was a queen, she had a greater number of attendants than the others and usually wore more beautiful clothes. Her little body was encased in the costliest fabrics, and three brass chests were scarcely sufficient to hold her jewels. When she was only eight years old, she had sixteen new dresses. A goldsmith furnished her with gloves, pins, combs and twelve dozen crescent-shaped buttons enamelled in black and white to trim her sleeves and decorate a coif of violet velvet. She had a golden girdle enamelled with white and red, and the King's silversmith provided her with many a yard of coloured velvet and taffeta, or Venetian satin and fine Holland linen. Perhaps these wrappings of golden damask and silver cloth, these hot velvet coifs and stiff sleeves, tired the little Queen, but she had a merry heart, and with one small hand holding up her heavy skirts she flung a ball or bowled a hoop with the other, and the corridors and gardens echoed with the patter of her eager feet and the joyful ripple of her laughter.

When they were tired of games, the children played with their animals. They had many pets, and when the weather was wet and they could not go out-of-doors they opened the gilded cages and lured the tame birds on to their fingers, or scampered up and down the long hall with their dogs. The latter were a never-failing source of joy, and between them the children had twenty-two little parlour dogs and four bull dogs, which were kept muzzled. They took a great interest in all animals and were never tired of seeing wild beasts and strange serpents from distant countries. The Dauphin had a little hind and once, to his great delight, some French nobles sent him two bears; he loved to take Mary to their cage and feed them with honeycombs, pealing with laughter and clapping his hands at their sticky paws and noses. From the bear-house the children would sometimes pass on to the stables. Nothing gave Mary greater pleasure than riding and hunting, and she and the Dauphin dearly loved their horses. Francis had three favourites called "Fontaine," "Enghein" and "Chastillon," but although Mary was careful to admire and pet them, she did not think them so beautiful as her own "Bravane" and "Madame la Réale."

As the court moved from place to place, the royal children frequently followed, enjoying the pageants which the cities prepared in their honour, devising fancy dresses for the balls in which the young lords and ladies delighted. The most exciting years for Mary were 1549 and 1550, when the French King and his Queen, Catherine de Medicis, were making a state entry into various cities. Mary's mother came from Scotland to see her and to take part in the different processions. The child eagerly looked forward to the visit, and wrote to her grandmother of

...the joyful news which I have received from the Queen, my mother, who has promised me that she will be here very soon to see you and me, which will be to me the greatest happiness I could desire in this world. I am so glad about it that my only thought now is to do my whole duty in all things and to study to be very good, in order to satisfy her wish to see me all that you and she desire....

Henry II of France at his state entry into Paris, 1549

It was a very grown-up letter for a little girl of eight, but Mary's life had been so cere-monious that she was old for her age, and even the King talked to her as though she were almost a woman. Her mother must have found her very much changed, and she was probably just as delighted with her daughter's graceful manners and dignified bearing in society, as she was with her pluck at the chase and her merriment when she played at hide-and-seek with the dogs in the palace corridors. Yet perhaps the frivolity and the constant gaiety at the French court troubled the child's mother, who knew that her little daughter's character would be influenced by her surroundings; for this reason she begged her brother, the Cardinal of Lorraine, to watch over Mary's religious training and to keep her constantly in his care. After this, when her mother had returned to Scotland, Mary was in close touch with her uncle, the Cardinal, who helped to strengthen her love of the Roman Catholic faith in which she had been brought up. He adored his niece and very soon Mary was happier with him than she was at court, for as she grew older, various things combined to annoy and worry her. Many a time she wept because the Dauphin's mother, Catherine de Medicis, was jealous of her popularity. By this time, too, the child's Scottish governess had returned to Edinburgh, and the French lady who had taken her place not only made mischief between her charge and the Queen-mother, but added petty domestic difficulties to her daily life. She grumbled when Mary wanted to give presents to her friends and servants, and even stole dresses from her wardrobe, so that when the young Queen looked for certain robes to give away, she could not find them, and wrote in great distress to her mother saying that people were beginning to think her mean.

In spite of her childish troubles, however, Mary grew prettier every day, and when she was fourteen years old she had become a beautiful, accomplished girl.

"She," wrote one of her biographers, "devoted great attention to acquiring some of the best languages of Europe, and such was the sweetness of her French that she was considered eloquent in it in the judgment of the most learned. Nor did she neglect Spanish or Italian, which she employed more for use than for show or lively talk. She understood Latin better than she could speak it. As for the graces of poetry, she had more from nature than art. She formed her letters well, and, what is rare in a woman, quickly. In the excellence of her singing, she profited greatly by a certain natural, not acquired, modulation of her voice. She played well on the cittern, the harp and the harpsichord. She danced excellently to music on account of her wonderful agility of body but yet gracefully and becomingly, for by quiet and gentle motion of her limbs she could express any harmony of strings."

When King Henry II found that his "daughter, the Queen of Scotland" had grown (as her uncle, the Cardinal, expressed it) "in beauty, wisdom and worth," he began to think of her wedding. Thus it was that on April 24th, 1558, the Queen of Scots was married to the Dauphin of France.

Never had Paris been so gay. Banners fluttered from the roofs of the houses. All who were rich enough to own tapestries hung them from their windows. Garlands of flowers were draped across the streets and every man, woman and child was in holiday attire. Early in the morning the city fathers clad in crimson and yellow, rode on their mules to the Cathedral of Nôtre-Dame. Behind them came a man of law in a velvet robe trimmed with yellow satin. The archers followed with bows in their hands, and the town-guard marched in the rear with musket and pike. In the Cathedral, they found the members of the *Parlement* already in their places, with the light from the painted windows gleaming on their scarlet robes, and the flames of countless candles glittering like pointed jewels in the still air. Costly needlework, embroidered in gold, hung from the walls, and chalices encrusted with precious stones glistened on the altars of every chapel.

Outside, the crowds, pressing one against the other, awaited the bridal procession. Mary was in the Archbishop's palace opposite the Cathedral, but the King was determined that all his subjects should see her, and so from the windows

of the great hall he had ordered a wooden platform to be built, twelve feet above the level of
the street. It looked more like a cloistered walk
than a platform, for the oak shelter was supported by Gothic arches, and overhead, the
wooden trellis-work was carved and painted to
look like vine leaves and their branches. There
could not have been a more perfect imitation of
the groined and vaulted roof of a Gothic aisle.
Near the door of the Cathedral, the covered way
expanded into an open pavilion. Its blue silk
roof, embroidered with the golden lily of France
and the rampant lion of Scotland, was stretched
over slender pillars. From this point the passage continued through the Cathedral door into
the nave and up the chancel, ending in another
pavilion carpeted with cloth of gold.

It was almost eleven o'clock when a fanfare
of trumpets warned the waiting people that the
bride was about to leave the Archbishop's palace.
When the last shrill note died away every eye
was turned towards the wooden colonnade.
There was a tense silence. Then something
stirred and under the arches marched the Swiss
halberdiers with the band of their regiment.
Behind came Mary's uncle, Francis, Duke of
Guise, robed from top to toe in cloth of gold.
Then came a bishop in all the glory of his embroidered vestments, walking with bowed head
behind his cross-bearer and followed by a train

of choir-boys holding lighted tapers in silver candlesticks. Minstrels, clad in scarlet and yellow, played softly on pipe, flute and tabor until the very air seemed alive with the sounds of singing-birds. The Scottish minstrels, too, were there with their bagpipes, and behind them came a hundred gentlemen of the court, eighteen bishops and abbots, six cardinals and the papal legate.

The people gazed in silence on this moving pageant, but those who were in the front of the crowd surged forward and a ringing cheer echoed through the Cathedral Square as the young Dauphin passed under the arches, led by his uncle, the King of Navarre, and followed by his little brothers. There were some who commented on the pale, delicate face and shook their heads, but most of the citizens turned away. They had eyes for no one but the bride.

With the King leading her by the right hand and the Duke of Lorraine by the left, Mary walked slowly towards the blue pavilion. She was beautiful beyond words, and when the people saw her a low murmur of admiration passed from lip to lip.

A chronicler of her day tells us:

She was dressed in a robe whiter than the lily, but so glorious in its fashions and decorations that it would be difficult, nay impossible, for any pen to do justice to its details. Her regal mantle and train were of bluish-grey cut velvet, richly embroidered with white silk and pearls. It was of a marvellous length, fully six *toises* (nearly twelve English yards), covered with precious stones and borne by young ladies. A priceless necklace hung round her throat and on her head she wore a golden crown encrusted with pearls, diamonds, rubies, sapphires, emeralds and other valuable jewels.

Like a glimmering fairy, she moved along the gallery, and as she passed a rosy light seemed to shine round her head, for in the middle of her crown blazed an enormous carbuncle.

When the procession had reached the first pavilion, the King drew from his finger a ring which he handed to the Archbishop, and in the presence of all the people, Mary Queen of Scots was married to the Dauphin of France.

As the royal pair passed through the great door of Nôtre-Dame to hear High Mass, the clear voice of a herald cried: "Largesse! Largesse! Largesse!" and baskets heaped with gold and silver coins were brought to the gallery and the money was flung to the crowd. Struggling and panting, the eager people grovelled for the coins until, at last, the danger to life became so great that voices were heard imploring the heralds to throw nothing more.

The wedding was over, but the festivities lasted for three days. There were balls, pageants and masques, but more fantastic than anything was the dinner given to the chief citizens at the Palais de Justice.

All round the great hall stood the statues of the French Kings. On the dais, at a marble table, sat the royal family and as each dish was handed to them music was played. Dancing followed, and then, before the astonished spectators, the doors of the Golden Chamber were flung open, and one by one came the seven planets to do homage to the bride and bridegroom. There was Mars in shining armour, Mercury in white satin with a golden girdle and spreading wings, Venus in soft light silks which fluttered as she moved. Then came twelve gilded wicker hobby-horses ridden by princes dressed in gold. Coaches carrying pilgrims were drawn through the long hall, and Mary who had always loved mummery and fancy dress, watched with eyes which were almost as bright as her jewels. She thought that the masters of the household had surpassed themselves, but something more was to follow.

Through the open doors, dipping and swaying before an artificial breeze, came a long train of ships, silver-sailed and draped with crimson velvet. On the deck of each there were two golden thrones, and as they passed the marble table, the King stepped on board, drawing the little bride to her place beside him. The Dauphin followed with his mother, and one by one the royal guests took their seats. Music whispered. The ships moved forward, still swaying softly, and the wedding party was carried out of sight.

Mary was married and the days of her childhood were over. Seated below the silver sail, she passed from the hall, a glittering animated figure, unconscious of the shadow which was hanging over her, little knowing that in four short years another ship would carry her away from France. She had left Scotland, a child of five, "full of cheer"; she was to return a widow of eighteen, burdened with sorrow. When, as a baby of nine months, she had wept at her coronation, people foretold a reign of tears. Mary fulfilled their prophecy, until a day came when she walked, dry-eyed, to the scaffold.

CHAPTER III

THE VOYAGE OF THE *BONAVENTURE*

[1553–4. Richard Chancellor seeks the north-east
passage and comes to Russia]

William was in the cabin, looking slightly green
but pretending that nothing was amiss. He was
off duty and had been lying down, and now he
was trying to make himself tidy. His hair was
ruffled. His short coat with the padded sleeves
and his flat leather hat were on the bunk and he
was making a valiant effort to manipulate the
points which attached his trunks to his hose,
but the motion of the ship flung him from one
side of the cabin to the other, so that dressing
was a lengthy process.

When he was ready, he went up on deck and
looked at the sky. A heavy bank of clouds in
the distance filled him with foreboding, and he
sat on a coil of rope and stared at the sea.

The water was grey and choppy, and a brisk
salt breeze was blowing, but the ships looked
beautiful with the wind in their sails and were
cutting through the waves, leaving long white
streaks behind them. There were three in the
fleet—the *Bona Confidentia*, a small vessel of
ninety tons, which was leading, the *Bona Esperanza* (the flagship), commanded by Sir Hugh
Willoughby, and the *Edward Bonaventure*, the

biggest of all, which had been William's floating home for the last eight weeks. Each had her own small pinnace and William gazed at them proudly, thinking that a finer set of ships had never sailed the sea. They were new, for the public had collected six thousand pounds to have them built, and they were fitted with all the latest devices even to their keels, which were covered with thin sheets of lead to prevent the "sea-worms" from boring through them. William was confident that such a fleet, with a captain-general like Sir Hugh Willoughby and a pilot like Master Richard Chancellor, could not fail to find the north-east passage. His eyes brightened when he thought of this great adventure, and forgetting his seasickness he jumped up and began to shout to the tune of a popular ballad: "Oh, what a surprise for the Spaniard-ho! Oh, what a surprise for the Portuguese!"

Like many of his elders he was jealous of the Portuguese and the Spaniards, jealous because the Portuguese were the first people to sail all the way round Africa and find a path to India, jealous because Master Christopher Columbus had discovered the new world of America for Spain and because a Spanish ship had sailed past South America into the Pacific Ocean, reaching India and the Spice Islands from the other side. Of course, Spain and Portugal were growing rich with their treasure and their trade, and they guarded their roads to the east with great care. William frowned when he thought about it, but laughed when he looked at the jaunty little vessels sailing north. If the English did not find a north-east passage to mysterious Cathay or the Indies, they might discover a new world, like Columbus, and bring fresh trade and wealth to their country. The idea filled him with delight and he threw back his head and carolled again: "Oh, what a surprise for the Spaniard-ho! Oh, what a surprise for the Portuguese!" until the mariners, who were busy about their various tasks, stood still scratching their heads and wondering what had happened to the pilot-major's page.

William could not help smiling when he looked at the mariners. It was difficult to believe that these dirty men, in their untidy canvas slops and woollen caps, could ever be elegant. Yet at the beginning of the voyage they had been as smart as possible, in sky-blue liveries, and as they were rowing the little boats which had towed the ships down the Thames, with cheering crowds on each side and the sick King waving from his window in Greenwich Palace, they had seemed almost as fine as the silk and velvet-clad gentlemen on the banks. But now the gay liveries were carefully packed away and would not see the light again until the ships arrived at some strange port, where

captain-general and pilot would doubtless want
to make a good impression. Even William had
put aside his tidy clothes. He knew the rules
of the ship. They were in Chancellor's cabin,
thirty-two of them written on a long sheet of
parchment, with a great red seal hanging from
it and the heading:

Ordinances, instructions and advertisements of and
for the direction of the intended voyage for Cathay,
compiled, made and delivered by the right worship-
full M. Sebastian Cabota Esquier, governour of the
mysterie and companie of the Merchants adventurers
for the discoverie of Regions, Dominions, Islands and
places unknowen, the 9 day of May, in the yere of our
Lord God 1553 and in the 7 yeere of the reigne of our
most dread soveraigne Lord Edward the 6, by the
grace of God, King of England, Fraunce and Ireland,
defender of the faith, and of the Church of England
and Ireland in earth supreme head.

It was a formidable heading and an equally
formidable set of rules followed. There were
laws for the captain, the master and the
mariners, for the surgeon, the steward and the
cook, for the merchants who had brought goods
for sale and barter in foreign lands, and general
regulations for the good conduct of everyone.
There was a rule that prayers and the Bible
should be read morning and evening, that anyone found dicing and card-playing should be
punished, and that no one was to be guilty of
conspiring, telling false tales or blaspheming.

William had once seen a mariner punished for swearing and had felt sorry for the wretched man, who was made to stand for over an hour in a conspicuous place, holding a marline-spike in his mouth. Confinement to the irons and sousing were mild punishments in comparison, and William had often watched a lazy seaman being ducked from the yard-arm and had tried not to laugh when he wriggled and spluttered, but he avoided looking at the mast when some offender was tied there with weights round his neck, moaning that his back was ready to break.

Proud of being Chancellor's page and nervous of the severity with which any offence was punished, William was determined to obey the rules. He could not, of course, remember them all by heart, but two were deeply imprinted on his mind and he always felt a little ashamed of himself when he recollected that his own misdemeanours had served to impress them. Once, at the beginning of the voyage when the ships were still within sight of Suffolk, he had been very seasick and, instead of carrying out his duties, had fallen asleep in the cabin. The following morning Chancellor had sent for him and sternly pointed to rule eleven. William had read with growing consternation:

Item, if any Mariner or officer inferiour shalbe found by his labour not meete or worthie the place that he is presently shipped for, such person may bee unshipped and put on lande at any place within the King's Majesties realme & dominion, and one other person more able and worthy to be put in his place....

William had spent some uncomfortable moments, fearing that the pilot-major would put him ashore. The second time that his attention had been drawn to a rule was quite different. He had been listening to stories of foreign lands and had suddenly said, "How I shall laugh when I see new people with strange customs and perhaps no clothes." And the officer to whom he had been talking had looked at him very solemnly but with a twinkle in his eye, and read aloud:

Item, every nation and region is to be considered advisedly, & not to provoke them with laughing, contempt or such like, but to use them with prudent circumspection, with al gentleness and curtesie....

and when he had thought the matter over, William came to the conclusion that Master Sebastian Cabot was right.

Looking across the water and meditating about this rule, he wondered what strange new countries the little fleet would reach and how soon Willoughby and Chancellor would find the hidden north-east passage. He was so busy with his thoughts that he did not notice how the wind had risen, and he was startled by the shouts of the mariners and the sudden tacking of the vessel. Jumping to his feet, he faced the storm and before he knew what had happened a wave broke across the deck, drenching him with spray. He staggered, gasping for breath, with bent head and every muscle taut, and as he did so the *Bona Esperanza* shot past on the crest of an immense breaker. In that instant William saw Sir Hugh Willoughby rush to the side of the ship, making a trumpet of his hands. He was evidently shouting something, but the roaring of the wind and the waves drowned his voice, and the flagship, as though she were the very spirit of the elements, sped towards the horizon and was soon out of sight. Buffeted by the wind and soaked to the skin, William clung to a rope, looking across the raging waters for the *Bona Confidentia* and the pinnaces. Far away, one tiny vessel was battling with the waves. With her mast almost touching the water, she rose and fell until at last she disappeared.

A friendly mariner helped William to the hatchway and he went below. He was feeling very ill and he sat on the floor of the cabin and leant against the partition, afraid to lie in one of the bunks lest the force of the waves should throw him out. The noise was deafening and he closed his eyes, trying to remember that it was all part of a great adventure which might bring glory to England as other adventures had brought glory to Spain and Portugal. He hummed feebly, "Oh, w-what a surprise for

the Sp-Spaniard," but the tune died away and
he could think of nothing but his last glimpse
of the *Bona Esperanza* as she was borne out of
sight and the little *Confidentia* disappearing in
the trough of the sea. He began to feel giddy.
He staggered to his feet, looking for his water-
bottle, and was flung violently across the cabin
with his head against the wooden edge of a
bunk. For a minute he saw one vivid scarlet
streak and then he seemed to be falling from
a great height into a pool of darkness.

William never quite knew what had happened.
When the storm had lulled, he was conscious of
people moving about him, but he was too dazed
to open his eyes, and when at last he came to
himself, he found that he was lying on a mattress on deck with his head bandaged and the
cool wind playing on his face. He sat up weakly,
asking questions, and learned that he had been
ill for several days. Then his heart sank, for he
knew that he must have neglected his duties and
he remembered rule eleven. Indeed, he was so
distressed that Chancellor himself came to
pacify him, laughingly assuring him that, apart
from the laws of good conduct, the only rule
which applied to an invalid was number
eighteen:

Item, the sick, diseased, weake and visited person
within boord, to be tendred, relieved, comforted and
holpen in the time of his infirmitie. . . .

The boy felt happier after this and before very long he was able to take off his bandages and carry out some of the light tasks which Chancellor set him. He worked as cheerfully as he could, but he was troubled about the fate of the other ships and it was obvious that Chancellor shared his anxiety. The pilot-major scanned the sea for a familiar sail and when the little page asked him if there was any hope, he patted his shoulder, saying "Wait till we reach the Wardhouse," and William took courage. He knew that Sir Hugh Willoughby had chosen the Wardhouse, a haven on the Norwegian coast, as a meeting-place in the event of the ships being dispersed in a storm, and he was impatient to reach it.

Unfortunately the Wardhouse was a forlorn hope. For seven days the *Edward Bonaventure* was anchored there and only a few small fishing boats cheered her loneliness. The *Bona Esperanza* was lost. The little *Confidentia* which had led the fleet so proudly and the two pinnaces, which had always reminded William of a pair of sea-birds, never came to the meeting-place. The *Edward Bonaventure* was all that remained of the gay little fleet.

As the days passed, William's heart grew very heavy. He sorrowed for the loss of his brave comrades and he felt miserable when he thought that the enterprise had failed. Three ships had set out to find the north-east passage and only one was left. Could she continue by herself? Could the *Edward Bonaventure* surprise the Spaniards and the Portuguese without the help of the other vessels?

He soon had an answer to his question. Chancellor summoned his men and with one voice they agreed to continue the voyage.

After this, life seemed to become one long adventure. The very sky was strange and new, for the ship had reached those northern climes where the sun shone at midnight. Darkness never fell and the sea sparkled brightly from one day's end to another. William was busy. He waited upon Chancellor at table, made notes of the voyage at his dictation and dreamed night and day of the north-east passage and the mysterious lands that the *Edward Bonaventure* was going to discover. Since he had seen the sun shining at midnight, he felt that nothing would surprise him. But he was wrong. The day came when Chancellor, steering across a great bay in the hope of finding the passage, put ashore in a strange land where the churches were scarlet, green and white with gilded domes, and the nobles wore long beards and pointed hats.

Standing at Chancellor's elbow and looking about him, William found it difficult to pre-serve the silence demanded of a page. He was longing to ask questions and was about to whisper: "Please is this Cathay?" when Chancellor turned to his companions, saying: "They tell me that we're in Muscovie, the land of a great emperor, called the Grand Duke Ivan Vassilivitch."

For a few minutes William was dumb with astonishment. He had heard of Muscovie, but to him and most Englishmen it was little more than a name, and none of his fellow-countrymen had ever been there. Had the *Edward Bonaventure* found a new world after all? The little page drew a deep breath. "It's a fairy tale," he cried. And even Chancellor laughed.

Living in such a fairy tale was a delightful experience for William and scarcely a day passed without some adventure. He wandered around the shores of the White Sea, visiting towns and villages. He peeped into the peasants' cottages and marvelled when he saw those great bearded men lying asleep on their stoves. He was entertained by the nobles, whom he learned to call *boyars*, and although he admired the jewelled *ikons* which hung high in the corners of each room, he thought the houses shabby and considered it a very ugly custom to fix wooden benches to the walls.

Eager for new sights, he was delighted when winter set in, although he knew that the northern seas were frozen and it would no longer be possible to seek the hidden passage. His brain was now busy with other plans. He felt sure that the *Edward Bonaventure* had brought glory to England by finding a sea-route to Muscovie. If she could carry home trading privileges, she would win even greater fame. This was evidently what Chancellor had in mind, for one day when a thin film of ice had covered all the pools and snow was falling, he sent for his page and bade him prepare for a journey. Full of excitement William ran hither and thither, packing clothes and sorting under-linen, polishing the great silver brooch which fixed the plume in Chancellor's hat and cleaning the scabbard of his sword. He guessed that his master was going to Moscow to visit the court of the great Russian emperor and ask that English merchants might trade in the cities.

Never had William enjoyed a journey so much. Muffled in fur rugs, he drove for hundreds of miles in a sledge, with the snow crunching under the horses' hoofs and long icicles hanging from the branches of the fir-trees. It amused him to sleep sometimes in a peasant's cottage and sometimes in the house of a *boyar*, but nothing delighted him so much as his arrival in Moscow, and the feast which the Grand Duke Ivan Vassilivitch gave in the Eng-lishmen's honour.

Ivan was evidently pleased with his English

Old Moscow

guests. He sat at the end of his golden court, dressed in a silver robe with a jewelled crown upon his head. Opposite sat the Englishmen with William standing behind Chancellor, in his best coat with the padded sleeves, a clean white *chimay* showing above his velvet doublet and his trunks and hose so carefully trussed that not a crease was visible. He gazed surreptitiously at Ivan's bearded face and looked out of the corner of his eye at the *boyars*, who were seated on each side of the hall at four tables with three steps leading to each of them.

The golden platters and the grand clothes of the serving-men, who changed three times during the meal, filled the page with amazement, but nothing astonished him so much as a very old custom. He noticed that before anyone began to eat, Ivan first made the sign of the cross upon his own forehead, then taking a slice of bread gave it to the chief guest in the room, while one of his stewards cried: "The Grand Duke of Muscovy, Emperor of Russia, Ivan Vassilivitch, doth give thee bread." Then all the guests arose, and only seated themselves as they were named. After this the gentleman usher of the Hall came in, followed by a hundred and forty serving-men, clad in golden robes, and the feast began.

William found it very tiring, for he could eat nothing until the others were served and the meal lasted for several hours. This, however, was his first experience of a Russian feast. As time passed he grew accustomed to the long courses, for he remained in the country until

Ivan the Terrible

the spring, travelling to many different towns, where Chancellor was always received with courtesy and entertained lavishly.

The page soon found that his duties were

becoming more interesting as he accompanied his master everywhere and had charge of the tablets, on which he noted which parts of the country were rich in tar and wax, which yielded furs, flax, hemp and other commodities. He was behind his master's chair when an embassy came to Moscow from Poland, and he helped Chancellor to remember the details, so that he might describe the visit in his notes.

Indeed, life grew more interesting from day to day, and William was almost sorry when the snow melted and he had to bid farewell to his Russian friends and journey once more to the shores of the White Sea.

By that time the port was free from ice and the *Edward Bonaventure*, freshly painted and careened, lay at anchor, awaiting the pilot-major. Peasants in sheepskin coats, fisher-folk with their nets and boats, and *boyars* in peaked hats and long fur-lined robes stood on the shore smiling and cheering as the little barque sped out to sea.

The adventure was over, and William turned away to answer a call from Chancellor. As the page came in, the pilot-major looked up with a document in his hand. It was a letter from Ivan Vassilivitch to Edward VI. William smiled. There was a question in his eyes as Chancellor gave him the key of his chest. Then he could contain himself no longer.

"Trade?" he asked, forgetting his manners. The pilot-major nodded. He was fond of the boy and liked his enthusiasm. "Aye," said he, "and this is what the Emperor Ivan says." He handed William a slate on which he had written a rough translation of part of the letter, and with glowing eyes the boy read:

Your countrymen...shall have their free Marte with all free liberties through my whole dominions with all kinds of wares to come and goe at their pleasure, without any let, damage or impediment, according to this our letter, our word and our seale which we have commanded to be under-sealed. Written in our dominion, in our citie and our palace in the castle of Mosco.

The *Edward Bonaventure* had found a road to Muscovie and was carrying special trading privileges back to England. William raised his head and his eyes looked very large and bright. The north-east passage was forgotten. Forgotten, too, was rule eleven and the decorum due to a master from his page. William brandished the slate in the air and skipped round the cabin. "Oh, oh, oh," he chanted, "what a surprise for the Spaniard! What a surprise for the Portuguese!"

CHAPTER IV

YOUR HONOUR'S SLAVE

[A.D. 1586. Ralph Fitch is the first Englishman to visit Burma]

Under the sparse shade of mango-tree and toddy-palm, the straggling lanes of the village were grass-grown and dusty. Broad, deep ruts broke the surface of the ground, where naked babies were crawling at will among pigs and poultry, and on the heaps of garbage, carelessly flung to rot in the sun, pariah dog and crow scratched for a meal. Here and there, a cream-coloured bullock with a double hump and long curved horns was tethered under a house, for the little bamboo dwellings were raised on posts, several feet above the ground, as a protection against snakes and floods.

They were picturesque houses, thatched with dried leaves or elephant grass and somewhat open in front, with yellow convolvulus climbing up the sides and bougainvillaea trailing along the roofs and drooping in long festoons over the walls. A visitor mounting the rickety steps to the platform in front, and peeping inside, would have seen a bare room with partitions of light matting, floors of split bamboo, and no furniture but a low table, scarcely six inches above the ground, some sleeping mats, and a child's cradle like a small open box swinging sideways on ropes of twisted grass attached to the roof-beams.

In a slow procession, the yellow-robed Buddhist monks were walking with downcast eyes through the village. Their bent heads were closely shaven, their feet were bare, and round their necks hung wooden begging-bowls supported by leather bands. Each of them carried a large fan made from the leaf of the talipat-palm, to shade his face lest his meditation should be disturbed by the sun or the sight of the village women combing their sleek black hair. Without asking or thanking for alms, they stopped before each house, and from lacquered baskets, kept for the purpose, the villagers dropped into the begging-bowls a cupful of boiled rice or some vegetables. The monks passed on, and behind, with large basins carefully held between their hands, walked the two little *kyaung thagale*, "sons of the monastery," who were learning to be monks and whose duty it was to collect food for those who had not joined the procession.

A stranger, borne by six men in a sort of litter made of cords and quilted cloth, gazed with the greatest interest at the proceedings, but the small, naked boy in the bullock-cart behind him looked on with respectful indifference. Ever since he had been a baby playing in the dust at his mother's door, he had seen the monks passing through the village on their daily round. He was used to the yellow-robed mendicants, accustomed, too, to the monastery at the gates of the village, which had excited the stranger's attention. The small boy liked to look at it, not because it was unusual but because he might, one day, go there to learn lessons, and because it was more beautiful and elaborate than the ordinary bamboo houses. He liked the teak-wood from which it was made, the gilded pea-cocks on the eaves and the curved and painted roofs which rose, one above another, and were decorated with fantastic carvings of those spirits which men called *nats*. Nevertheless, it surprised him to see how the stranger walked round the building staring, counting the roofs and examining each thick post, which supported the platform, passed through the balustrade and terminated in a carved and painted head.

To the child, the stranger's clothes, and indeed the man and all his pursuits, were infinitely more surprising than the monastery and its simple yellow-robed inmates. This pale, bearded foreigner did not wear a bright silk scarf round his hair like the men of Pegu or the villagers on a holiday, but his head was crowned by a high black hat with a bunch of curling feathers at the side. Instead of a jacket he wore a little cape, hanging from his shoulders over a doublet, slashed and embroidered in silk, and instead of the Burmese *lungyi* or short coloured skirt, twisted round the loins, he had skin-tight hose gartered with silk ribbons and puffed at the thigh into slashed trunks. Sometimes he wore a stiff ruff round his throat, but he pulled it off when the heat of the sun made him tired, and his neck underneath was as pale as the milk of a goat.

He excited considerable attention in the village, and when the procession of monks had passed, men, women and children crowded round the litter staring at the occupant and impeding the progress of the luggage cart, which lumbered behind, so that the driver had to shout and crack his whip.

Like every other child, the boy in the bullock-cart had a name, but because he was employed by the stranger to run errands, guard the luggage and keep the flies off the bullock, he modestly described himself as "*Kyúndaw*," which means "Your honour's slave"; and, to his great amusement, Kyúndaw he became, till the terms of his service were at an end, for the stranger's tongue was shy of foreign names and his memory weak.

Kyúndaw looked neither modest nor slavish as he drove through the village. He sat in perky nakedness by the driver, with a string of beads

round his little pot-belly and in his mouth a
quid made from the clipping of an areca nut,
wrapped in a leaf of the betel-vine with a touch
of white lime at each end. Every now and then
he spat casually but accurately into a rut in the
road, and cracked a whip which neither hastened
nor slackened the pace of the bullock.

A Burmese lady travelling

Jogging after the litter with a cloud of dust
rising behind, he passed through the wooden
gates in the stockade which surrounded the
village and followed the white road to Pegu.
His eyes were on his master, who was continually stopping the bearers, climbing out of
the litter and looking about him, even when
nothing was passing. To Kyúndaw this seemed
a little foolish, for teak and eng-wood, mango
and pepper tree were common enough, and

there was nothing remarkable about the rice fields, flooded, green, and at different stages of growth. He smiled lazily at the stranger's interest in the thatched cupboards by the roadside, where a wayfarer might quench his thirst by dipping a long-handled coco-nut cup into the water-jars inside them. When his master stopped for the third time, the small boy shrugged his shoulders and confided in the bullock that the ways of foreigners were strange, but the great beast plodded along, whisking its tail indifferently, as much as to say, "Why not? There are many fleas on a dog's back!" And Kyúndaw began to wish that Pegu were not so far away.

He had never been to that golden city and although he was an easy-going little fellow, who seldom showed any excitement, he could not help chewing rather faster and spitting with greater relish when he remembered that he was going for the first time in the company of a stranger, and that in the circumstances he would be treated by young and old with the respect due to a foreigner's attendant.

As the bullock-cart pushed slowly forward in the dust, he imagined himself passing through the city gates to the guest-house, politely waving aside the proffered help of the onlookers as he unloaded his master's goods, tethering his bullock under the veranda and dismissing importunate advice with a wave of the hand and a pitying "Show the King of the crocodiles what to do in the water."

He saw himself seated cross-legged outside the guest-house, surrounded by an admiring crowd who would ask questions about the stranger, desiring to know his name, where he came from, and where he was going. Knowing nothing about his master except that he was kind, wore strange clothes and had inquisitive habits, Kyúndaw proceeded to invent a tale of a king in disguise, but the idea reminded him that he might possibly see a real King in Pegu and his thoughts drifted into other channels.

He had heard of the King's palace with its walls of gilded wood, its golden pagoda roofed with silver tiles and the surrounding buildings where he kept his elephants of war. At the thought of these animals Kyúndaw chewed vigorously. He had always cherished an ambition to see a white elephant, and although the King of Pegu only used black ones in battle, Kyúndaw knew that he had four white ones, which had given him his name, "The King of the White Elephants." The little boy wondered whether his master would be permitted to see these magnificent beasts and planned to follow him, wherever he went, with the excuse that so exalted a personage might want an extra fan or fly-whisk or painted sunshade, which his slave would carry.

Dreaming blissfully of the tales which he would tell when he returned to the village, Kyúndaw was startled to find himself almost at the gates of Pegu, and with an astonished grunt he dived into the back of the cart and hastily untying his own bundle began to put on his best clothes, until in skirt, jacket and silk scarf he was like a grown-up in miniature.

The city lay in a pool of sunshine, and as Kyúndaw followed his master's litter through the gates, he saw that it was divided into two parts, an old town, where the merchants lived and sold their goods in a great market, and a new city behind the walls of which the King lived in his palace, surrounded by his nobles, and guarded by sentinels in gilded turrets.

The merchant-city was humming with life. Water-carriers passed up and down, with terra-cotta jars slung from bamboos on their shoulders. Pedlars with baskets of coco-nuts on their backs walked slowly among the crowds, crying their wares and pushing past the melon-sellers whose green fruit was sliced to show the fresh pink pulp inside. Sometimes a lady, reclining in a painted bullock-gharry and attended by slaves, waved her fan and ordered one of her women to buy her a tit-bit, which some man was cooking in a charcoal fire on the tray on his head. Goatherds drove their flocks from house to house, milking them when the servants came out with their jars, and the air was hot, dusty and heavy with the sweet, pungent scents of the East.

Kyúndaw stared with amazement at the fine bamboo dwellings, for each had a brick ware-

An Eastern market-place in the sixteenth century

house where the merchant stored his goods. He tried not to look astonished but to preserve the air of experienced boredom which a great man's servant should wear, and he flicked some beggars with his whip when he saw inquisitive eyes peering at the luggage in the cart. A crowd was gathering round the litter, and it was with difficulty that the little procession pushed its way through the bazaar. Girls seated at their stalls, enamelling their faces and throats with yellow powder mixed with water, ceased gossiping to stare at the litter. Merchants left their piles of scarlet cotton and white cloth to point with their chins at the stranger, asking "Who is he?" Spice-sellers leaned from their scented booths, shouting to one another, and even the eight brokers of Pegu, who were bound by law to sell a foreign trader's goods at the price which they were worth, came hurrying up to the bearers, pretending to clear the way, but peeping under the awning of the litter and hastily counting the boxes in the bullock-cart.

Kyúndaw, a little afraid lest thieves should pilfer something, was relieved when his master drew near to the new city and, crossing a bridge over the moat where crocodiles swam, passed through the gates to a small guest-house.

It was disappointing that no one would believe the story of a king in disguise, and humiliating that the bearers sent Kyúndaw to bed in the bullock-cart under the veranda, so that he could not even lie on a sleeping-mat at his master's door, though he could hear through the thin bamboos how the stranger groaned when he grew stiff from sitting on the floor and how his goose-quill scratched as he added sheet after sheet to those endless notes which he had been making whenever he had stopped his litter.

Gradually Kyúndaw's eyelids drooped and before he had time to think or to grumble it seemed to be morning again, and he grew slowly conscious of the lowing of the bullock and the voices of the bearers preparing the litter. He listened drowsily for a few minutes, but when he heard them discussing an early visit to the white elephants, sleep deserted him and he shot out of the bullock-cart like a jack-in-the-box.

Armed with a painted parasol and a palm-leaf fan, he stationed himself on the veranda. The bearers laughed and motioned him away, saying that the master would take no luggage to the enclosure, so that boy and bullock-cart could remain behind. But Kyúndaw was firm. A proverb of his country said, "In the forest of soft-woods the castor-oil plant is King." Kyúndaw had a fan and a parasol, the bearers had nothing but their litter. Kyúndaw would not move.

Indeed when the stranger came out and saw the quaint little figure in the elaborate grown-up garments with a fan almost as big as itself, he gave a hoarse chuckle and told Kyúndaw to sit in the litter beside him.

Ignoring the shrugs of the bearers and dexterously avoiding the surreptitious kick from a bare foot, the boy jumped up beside his master, and swinging his body slowly backwards and forwards, began to use his fan. He felt proud of his position, so proud that he scarcely noticed the broad streets which led from gate to gate, the tiled wooden houses with coco-nut trees at each door, nor the crowds which stood outside the walls and moats surrounding the gilded palace. He only remembered that he was the servant of a grand stranger who was about to visit the King's white elephants. That he did not know his master's name or business was a matter of no importance. Kyúndaw basked in reflected glory.

At the gates of the palace he stepped out of the litter and, still vigorously fanning, followed his master to a hall beyond which he saw four houses so brightly gilded from roof to floor that they gleamed in the sun till his eyes were dazzled. As he was watching, the door of the largest house was thrown open and out came ten men playing drums, singing songs and clashing cymbals. In his enthusiasm, Kyúndaw stopped fanning his master and began to beat time, clapping his hands and stamping his feet. Just as the musicians passed, an immense white elephant stepped majestically from its gilded house and raising its trunk in the air, began to trumpet.

Kyúndaw dropped on to his knees and touched the ground with his forehead, but he peeped out of one eye and saw the great beast moving with lumbering tread towards the river. Over its head, eight men carried a canopy of cloth of gold, and behind came a Peguan gentleman, richly dressed and with a silver basin in his hand. One by one, the doors of the houses opened and from each came an elephant, preceded by musicians, attended by bearers and followed by a noble with a silver basin. The rare white beasts were going down to the river to bathe, and the gentlemen with the shining bowls were to have the honour of washing their feet.

With his forehead bowing to the ground Kyúndaw watched them. As each one passed the stranger and his small attendant, it trumpeted. Kyúndaw listened, spell-bound and miserable. To the little boy whose ear was trained to catch every whisper at the village-well and every noise in the jungle, the sound was scornful and mocking. He wriggled and raised both eyes as high as he dared. The last elephant was passing. Slowly, heavily it raised its great feet, trumpeting loudly. As it passed Kyúndaw's prostrate form, it stopped for a minute, waved its trunk, picked up the palm-leaf fan and with an air of supreme contempt cast it into the dust. Kyúndaw trembled. The little pink eyes of the elephant looked at him and between the half-closed lids he saw a gleam of mockery

Scrambling to his feet, the child watched the

procession until it reached the river. Then he looked at the strangely-dressed figure beside him and his lip trembled. He had thought it was a privilege to be a foreigner's servant and carry a palm-leaf fan, but now he knew that no honour was as great as the washing of a white elephant's feet.

He picked up the despised fan and began to use it in a desultory way. His heart was heavy with humbled pride, and as he passed in the litter from temple to monastery, storehouse to shop, with his master writing on tablets at every stopping-place, he could think of nothing but the contemptuous trumpeting of a white elephant and the scornful glance from a small pink eye.

If anyone had told him that he had been serving Ralph Fitch, the first English merchant to visit Burma, he would have felt no reflected glory. He would not have been impressed if he had heard that Ralph Fitch, armed with his notes on eastern lands and goods, would one day help to form a famous company of merchants, who would trade with the King of Pegu and the East Indies.

The little boy of the bullock-cart had lost all interest in foreign masters. He wanted to be "Kyúndaw" to a white elephant.

CHAPTER V

THE EAGLE OF THE NORTH

[A.D. 1591. The escape of Hugh Roe O'Donnell from Dublin Castle]

The wind had a thousand moods that night. It slid down the hills, kissing the tree tops and dancing over the lake until the surface of the water was flecked with a million rippling footprints. It whispered a lullaby, crooning round the straw-thatch of the little hut and playfully puffing the smoke from the peat fire back through the hole in the roof. It moaned, crying fretfully round the turf walls, caressing them with the feeble, fluttering touch of a sick girl until with sudden petulance it shrieked aloud, and in a frenzied outburst of rage rushed from hill to hill, driving the snow before it till the valley was hidden in a whirling mass of white flakes, and every tree in Glenmalure bent to the ground, groaning and creaking. With a shuddering wail, it tore at the straw-covered roof, beating against the walls as though it would crush them and with one swift rush carry the tiny shelter into the swirling waters of the lake below.

To Bridget, it seemed as though the *Sidhe*, the fairy Host of the Air, were riding in a long, mad race among the hills, and she crossed herself, whispering a prayer for wanderers. The cold made her shiver, and she pulled her blue homespun cloak round her shoulders and threw more peat on the ashes, wishing that she could sleep like her parents, who lay huddled together on the ground with their feet towards the fire, or the little dun cow whose silky sides moved rhythmically up and down as her sweet warm breath mingled with the smell of the peat.

The fire glowed and Bridget stirred it with a stick, and kneeling stooped over it, blowing the ashes till the grey flakes brightened to a ruddy gold and made the light flicker and dance over her face. She saw pictures in the fire, fairy folk who tossed white arms above their heads, twisting and turning till they fell to pieces and formed themselves into little fiery ladies, like those of Fiach MacHugh's household, with long fringed mantles and fold upon fold of white linen standing out from their heads like cheeses. She saw flowers, too, whose curling petals faded when the flames burned low, and strange monsters whose changing shapes crumbled to dust as the peat broke.

Picture after picture quivered in the glimmering heart of the fire, and as Bridget moved, leaning on one elbow and tucking her feet under her cloak, the little dun cow sighed, turning its head towards her and gazing with large sad eyes into her face. The child stroked the wet nose softly and, still staring at the fire, fell to thinking of the tales which she had been told of the English soldiers, who stole the Irish cattle and burned the fields of those who rebelled against them. "Soldiers!" she muttered, and her lip curled. "Soldiers, who fear to walk barelegged, yet laugh at the warm Irish mantles! Soldiers, who chafe their horses' backs with saddles and can only mount by a stepping-stone or a stirrup." Then she thought of the fighting Irishmen of Glenmalure, of Fiach MacHugh, who could always drive the English away from his mountains and winding valleys. She had seen him marching and riding among the hills, with his horsemen following in quilted leather coats with long-bladed daggers at their hips, each with three horses and a lad to lead them and to carry the spears. She could see them now, with the gallowglasses on foot behind them. Bridget stirred the fire and smiled, for the gallowglasses were the pride of her race, tall strong men in shirts of mail and metal skull-caps, who fought with battle-axes and were a terror to the enemy. Each had his boy with a sheaf of darts, and behind them all marched the kernes, lithe men, lightly clad in shirts and short coats, lightly armed with sword, bow and arrows, fleet of foot, swift of action, with eyes quick to spy out a wood or a bog from which they could fight unobserved. Many a time she had seen them winding their way across the hills, for Fiach MacHugh was ever ready to lead a rebel or harbour a refugee who would not recognise English Elizabeth, nor say the prayers, nor obey the laws of the Pale.

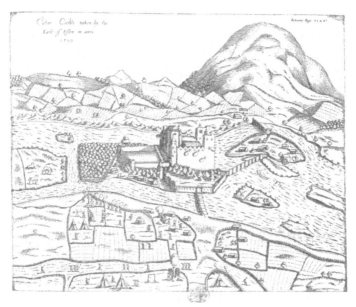

Fighting in Ireland, 1599

Bridget's eyes darkened when she thought of the Pale, that English stronghold in the midst of her country, where Irishmen were learning foreign ways, where soldiers and high sheriffs walked as though they had bought the four provinces of Erin. Though Bridget was only a cowherd who had never left the hills of Glen-malure, though Queen Elizabeth was scarcely more than a name to her and she had never seen an Englishman, the conquest of Ireland was a living terror to her. She knew that many a brave gallowglass had never returned from battle. She heard tales, too, from the people who rode along the bridle paths to Fiach Mac-Hugh's castle, and when she carried her milk pails to the castle dairy, she stayed to gossip and to listen. Many a story she had heard of a battle or a raid, of Irish chiefs who had been made earls by the English and were drifting away from the old customs of the land. She heard stories of the burning of fields and homes, of boys taken from their parents as hostages and sent to England to be brought up as English, wearing the English clothes, speaking the English tongue, praying English prayers; boys, kept as sureties lest their parents should rebel, nurtured in foreign ways lest they should follow in their fathers' footsteps.

There were hostages, too, kept by Sir John Perrot, the English Lord Deputy, in Dublin Castle, so near to their own homes and yet so far away. Bridget stirred uneasily and stretched her thin hands to the fire as she thought of the wind howling round the great stone walls which hid the captives. Young Hugh O'Donnell was there, Red Hugh, whose fame had spread from province to province until all Ireland sang his praises. Graceful he was and tall, with hair as red as burnished copper and a wisdom and knowledge beyond his years. He was beloved by many, for among his foster-fathers were the chiefs of his own clan and those of others.

The Lord Deputy leaving Dublin Castle

Bridget's little pointed face had a brooding look when she thought of him. His clan lived far away in the north-west corner of Ireland, but she had heard of him and believed with every shepherd on the mountains, every young man and maid in Glenmalure, that he was the youth of whom St Caillin foretold long ago:

There will come a man glorious, pure, exalted,
Who will cause mournful weeping in every territory.
He will be the god-like prince.
And he will be King for nine years.

There were those who wept for him now. Bridget lay down with her hands behind her head and her back pressed snugly against the warm little cow, thinking. She remembered the day when she had first heard of Red Hugh. It was at a feast one summer. Fiach MacHugh was entertaining his guests, and Bridget had come down from the mountain with butter wrapped in cool dock leaves and a pail of that curdled cream which the Irish ladies loved. The feast was spread under the blue sky, the food on a high table, and the guests on benches, or mounds of hay with piles of green fern before them, where they could set their platters or wipe their knives. She remembered how soft the blue and brown mantles looked against the grass and how the whole lawn was a moving pageant of colour, for many of the men wore scarlet breeches and stockings, which made a brilliant contrast to the wide hanging sleeves of their saffron shirts. She remembered how they tossed back their long hair when they talked, and how gracefully the women moved, turning proud heads framed in white linen, lifting round white arms that were loaded with bangles. There were young girls, too, talking and laughing with the youths. Their eyes were merry and they shook their heads and shrugged their shoulders till their long ringlets, looped with ribbons, danced like autumn leaves in the wind.

Running hither and thither with ewers and platters were the bare-legged serving-men in yellow shirts, chattering, hurrying, eager that everyone, from the chiefs to their dogs, should be happy. And Bridget had slipped shyly from one guest to another, passing the bowls of cream, and welcomed by Fiach MacHugh and his lady with the same smile that they gave to their guests.

It was after the feast that she had heard the story of Red Hugh. The bard sat in the place of honour, beside him his harper and the fair-haired *reacaire* who sang or recited his rhymes. The bard made a sign with his hand, and through the still air the strings of the harp hummed with the music of the chase and the *reacaire* sang the song of Hugh O'Donnell.

He sang of a youth, comely as the moon and straight as a young tree, who hunted with his friends round Rathmullan, till weary with sport they had climbed to a castle on the shore. He sang of Hugh's foster-father who lived at the castle and opened its doors to this child, as dear to him as his own son. He sang of the meeting between the two. Then the music changed and through the strings of the harp rippled the sound of the sea, and the *reacaire* sang of a fair merchant-ship which swept, white-sailed, up Lough Swilly and lowered her anchor under the castle walls. Her pennons were fluttering gaily

and the coracle rocking beside her brought a
merchant crew ashore. "Ho, gentles!" they
cried. "Here's sweet Spanish wine and sack
for sale. Come buy. Come buy." Through the
harpstrings pattered the sound of hurrying feet,
and the *reacaire* sang of Rathmullan and how
the folk hastened down to the shore, buying the
sack and carousing. Then the butlers came from
the castle, saffron-shirted, bare-legged, with
their long hair lifting in the wind. "Ho, merchants! Ho! We would have wine for the
castle guests." Then softly the harp played,
alluring and sly, and in tones smooth as silk
came the answer: "The wine has been bought.
There is no more for sale! Bring the guests of
the castle aboard, for the captain alone has wine
on his table." The harp throbbed and wailed as
the *reacaire* sang how Red Hugh O'Donnell,
the pride of the land, took a boat with some
friends and rowed to the vessel, climbing the
ladder and leaping aboard. The rough hands of
sailors were stretched out to help him. The
smooth hands of merchants drew him down to
the cabin. The white wine sparkled in goblets
of silver as Red Hugh caroused with his friends
and the captain. The harper's fingers plucked
fiercely at the strings and the music sobbed and
wailed like the keening of women at a wake,
while the *reacaire* sang how the hatch was
fastened, the anchor drawn up and the ship

sped away from Lough Swilly. Then all the O'Donnells, O'Neills and MacSweenies wept for Red Hugh, the Eagle of the North. They rowed out in boats and they stood on the shore, stretching their arms and calling his name. Ransoms were offered and pledges were given, but Red Hugh O'Donnell had never come home. Through the strings of the harp fluttered the sound of a bird's wings beating against a cage, and all the guests on Fiach MacHugh's lawn were silent, thinking of young O'Donnell, a captive in Dublin Castle. But Bridget had crept away, back to the little turf cabin on the hill, and her heart had never ceased beating for the red-haired youth whom the English had stolen.

She turned on her side and looked again at the dying fire. There were no pictures now, only a soft red glow which made the shadows on the wall dim and flat. Outside the wind whispered helplessly. The storm had passed and the silence in the hut was broken only by the soft breathing of the dun cow and the rustle of Bridget's parents as they moved the bundles of straw beneath their heads. The little girl yawned and stretched her arms, waiting drowsily for sleep and blinking at the crack of the door lest dawn should creep in unawares.

For a long while she lay dozing, half awake and half asleep, until something stole across her

dreams. At first she thought it was a light foot-
fall and a voice softly calling. She sat up and
listened. From the mountain came a faint cry
like the wail of an animal in pain. She heard it
once, twice. Then she stole to the door and,
lifting the wooden latch, pushed open the top
half and leaned out. A shower of water drops
fell from the roof on to her hair and the snow
stretched before her, a white waste, pure and
unbroken, growing brighter as the day began to
dawn. The cry came again and she looked about
her, seeking a lost animal which some careless
shepherd or cowherd had left out all night. But
she could see nothing on the bare hills and
nothing at the edge of the wood.

Faintly and wearily came the voice again and
with a pitiful "Oh, poor thing," Bridget pulled
her cloak over her head and went bare-footed
into the snow. She had heard a human voice.

She made a shell of her hands, lilting "Where
are you? Where?" as she sped down the hillside, and just where the hidden bridle path was
flanked by a wooden fence and a group of rocks
she heard the answer "Here." Scrambling over
the snow-covered stones, she slid to the other
side. There stood a man, gaunt as a mountain
goat, with the water dripping from his clothes
and his shoes torn. He pushed Bridget towards
a cave, where the shepherds used to take refuge
from storms, and whispering fiercely "Get them

An Irish Chief with his attendants

food while I go to Fiach MacHugh," he leapt down the hillside and disappeared.

With fear in her heart Bridget stooped and crawled into the cave. Two boys lay there, pale as the snow outside. Their linen shirts and short light coats were frozen to their bodies. Their cloth stockings were torn to ribbons and not the vestige of a shoe remained on their bleeding feet. They had no cloaks, but one had tied a light strip of plaid round his head to protect his ears and although he was almost fainting, his jaw moved, chewing some leaves. Neither boy could raise himself, but the younger with the plaid round his head, whispered, " Art's dying," then closed his eyes and seemed not to mind what was happening.

Covering them with her mantle, Bridget crawled out of the cave and ran like a frightened deer to the hut, calling, "Help me, mother, help me! Quick."

Sending her parents with peat, straw and a tinder-box, she milked the cow and sped down the hill, with her pail on one arm and a rough sheepskin rug on the other.

At the edge of the cave her parents had made a fire and were chafing the boys' frozen limbs. The younger sipped a little of Bridget's milk, but the elder fell heavily back against her shoulder and, with a little shiver, she knew that he was dead.

They rolled the younger in the sheepskin, pulling off his wet yellow shirt and covering him with Bridget's mantle, and they heated milk over the peat fire, urging him to swallow it, but his mind was wandering and he kept whispering, "Put one arm round my neck, Art, and the other round Phelim's. Now walk." Then fretfully, "My feet. Something's happened to my feet."

With fingers which were growing stiff, Bridget and her mother rubbed the boy's arms and legs, until they heard the welcome sound of voices and into the cave came Fiach MacHugh and his servants. They carried baskets made of reeds and they pulled out beer and bread and warm home-spun blankets, fringed at the edges. They fed the living boy, and crossed the dead one's arms over his breast, shaking their heads and murmuring, "Another O'Neill." Then they made a stretcher from the fence by the rocks and, spreading their cloaks over it, carried the sick boy to the woods, saying, "The deserted hut is the safest place in Glenmalure."

Bridget watched them with tears in her eyes, but she smiled her thanks to Fiach MacHugh, who wrapped her mantle round her and said, "I've a little red calf for you, Bridget, and at the next lambing you shall take your choice."

When he had gone, she ran back to the turf cabin, fetched three rush-lights and sat in the

cave by the body of Art O'Neill until the priest
and Fiach returned and buried him in a lonely
grave on the hill.

Afterwards, Bridget went every day to the
hut in the woods, taking with her a small cake
baked over the peat, a bowl of new milk and
sometimes a strip of linen for a bandage, which
her mother had woven, and as she crossed
the threshold she thought of the old proverb,
"Three slender things on which the world de-
pends: the slender stream of milk from the
cow's dug into the pail; the slender blade of
green corn upon the ground; the slender thread
over the hand of a skilled woman."

When Fiach MacHugh's servants were away,
or his lady at home and himself busy, Bridget
would sit with the stranger, washing and bind-
ing his feet and giving him warm milk or beer
from Fiach's jewelled goblets. He still lay with
his head wrapped in a scarf and his hands
bound in linen, but Bridget could see that his
eyes were large and grey, his skin as clear and
white as milk and his lips red and as delicately
curved as the petals of a rose. He talked to her
sometimes, but she was too shy to answer, so he
let her be, and watched as she moved about the
hut, straightening the blankets and blowing up
the fire.

One evening, when he was almost well, she
saw horses at the door, and her heart told her

that he was going. She heard him talking to Fiach, laughing a little, but troubled and excited.

"How did you do it?" asked Fiach, and he answered, "Phelim would come to see us. They let him in. And one day he brought us a rope and a file. When the guard was at dinner, Art filed off my chains and we carried the rope to a sewer which led to the moat. Henry O'Neill went first, then Art and I followed. We dropped into the moat, but a stone fell on Art's head and hurt him and so we could only move slowly." He paused for a minute and sighed. "We climbed up the bank, and my horse-boy met us and we went through the streets of Dublin; nobody seemed to notice that we were wet and muddy, for it was raining. When it was dark we lost Henry and went on alone. We climbed the fences round the city and came to Slieve Roe. Then it snowed and we walked and walked for two days, but Art had been so long in prison that he could not go fast. Besides, his head was hurt. When we reached Glenmalure, he could not move and we put his arms round our shoulders and the horse-boy and I tried to carry him. You know the rest. I sent Phelim to find you. I knew that Fiach MacHugh would never desert an O'Donnell."

Bridget's heart leapt. She gazed at the door of the hut. Fiach and his lady came out, supporting the stranger between them. The boy was wearing a blue fringed mantle. His feet were still bandaged, but his hands were free and he had taken the scarf from his hair, which glowed like burnished copper in the evening sun.

Bridget sprang to the horse's head and held the bridle as they lifted Red Hugh to its back. He took the reins and looked down smiling as the child knelt on the ground and tied the bandage more securely round his foot. "I did not know you," she said, and a crimson flush dyed her cheeks.

Red Hugh stooped from his horse and, putting his hand under her chin, tilted her face till her eyes looked into his. Then he kissed her lightly on the forehead. "He is thrice blessed who gives to a stranger," he said and rode away to the north.

Bridget watched him and her eyes were as bright as the evening star. "He will go home," she whispered, "and his father and the people will make him The O'Donnell, the chief of all. He will stand on the rath with horseman, gallowglass and kerne around him, and they'll give him the straight white wand, and he will turn about that all may see him and know that he will walk in the paths of justice, and that the straightness of his conduct and the whiteness of his heart are as the wand which they have given him."

She turned away and walked up the mountain, for Red Hugh was out of sight. One by one the stars crept into the sky, and the wind among the tree tops nodded good-night to a drowsy world. From the half-door of the little turf hut the light glowed, welcome and red, and a smell of peat was blown down the hill. On the threshold Bridget paused, making the sign of the cross. Then she went in and, closing the upper and lower parts of the door, stood with her back against them.

"The eagle of the north has flown," she said.

But her mother did not answer. She was crooning softly as she spun, and above the low humming of the wheel Bridget heard the rune of hospitality:

> I met a stranger yestreen:
> I put food in the eating place,
> Drink in the drinking place,
> Music in the listening place;
> And in the sacred name of the Triune
> He blessed myself and my house,
> My cattle and my dear ones.
> And the lark said in her song:—
>   often, often, often
> Goes the Christ in the stranger's guise;
>   often, often, often
> Goes the Christ in the stranger's guise!

CHAPTER VI

POCOHONTAS, THE LITTLE TOMBOY

[A.D. 1607–13. Captain John Smith and the early
planters in Virginia]

Mataoka was twelve years old, but because she
was such a madcap and so much more like a
boy than a girl, all the people of her tribe called
her Pocohontas, which meant "little tomboy."

To-night she certainly looked boyish, for she
carried a bow and some arrows. She had hidden
her long black hair and the coral band round
her forehead under a fur cap, her white deerskin cloak and short leather skirt did not reach
her knees, and her copper-coloured legs were
bare save for a pair of fur-lined moccasins,
beautifully decorated with porcupine quills and
bound to her feet by the dried sinews of some
animal.

She had been out alone, and now the sun had
set and she ran along the banks of the Pamunkey
River, flipping her fingers at the fireflies which
flickered among the trees, and uttering long
shrill cries to scare the wild beasts, whose eyes
were gleaming in the darkness like little green
lamps.

A bend in the river revealed Werowocomoco,
her village. It stood in a clearing of the forest,
with bare fields for Indian corn and tobacco on

each side, and behind it a thick tangle of briars, raspberry bushes and vines spreading among the birch and maple trees. Some of the squaws had lighted a fire to scare the animals and, as she ran shouting through the forest, Pocohontas could see the shadows dancing across the wigwams to the little mounds of earth which covered the baskets where grain had been stored for the winter.

The wigwams stood near together, but there were not many of them, for the Powhatans, like most of the Algonquin Indians, lived at close quarters, making each house large enough for ten or twenty families. The low, oblong buildings were neatly fashioned with a framework of pointed stakes, filled in with branches and reeds, and the round roofs were covered with matting woven from dried rushes. The friendly glow of the firelight shone through the open doorways, and from a hole in each roof the smoke rose in long straight streaks, which were just visible in the darkening sky.

There was very little difference between the shape and size of each house, but Pocohontas could easily distinguish her own because it was higher than the others. Her father, Wabunsonacook, was chief of the Powhatans, so his wigwam was built, like the Council Chamber, on a mound.

The little girl stopped shouting and running

as soon as she reached the fields and began to pick her way carefully. The earth was still hard and bare, but later the green shoots of the tobacco plant would appear above the ground, and Pocohontas thought of them with reverence. Tobacco was a sacred weed. She had known this ever since she was a tiny papoose, when her mother, puffing the fragrant blue smoke from a pipe, sent her to sleep with tales of the great spirits who lived above the sky. In the days when there was peace among men and animals, the great spirits sometimes visited the earth. One of them had brought tobacco to the Redskins. He had come down from the sky to hunt, and when he was weary he made a fire at the edge of a forest and lay down to sleep. But while he was sleeping an evil spirit found him and pushed him so near to the fire that his hair began to burn and he awoke. Springing to his feet, he rushed flaming through the forest and, wherever a charred strand of hair fell to the ground, a tobacco plant grew.

Thinking of the story, Pocohontas reached the village. A faint smell of tobacco greeted her; she knew that supper was over and that the braves were seated in the wigwams smoking and telling old tales of war and hunting. She smiled at the squaws who were tending the fire, and with a bound worthy of a tomboy leapt into the chief's wigwam.

It looked friendly and comfortable after the dark forest. Warm skins covered the walls, reed mats were spread on the floor, and hand-woven baskets with gay borders held the squaws' collection of feathers, porcupine quills, needles of bone and thread made of bears' gut. Poco-hontas glanced from left to right, greeting the members of her father's family, who were housed in small open compartments on each side of the central passage. Some of the squaws were already asleep on the floor or on wooden shelves spread with furs, and their fat little papooses were in birch bark cradles lined with moss and suspended by reindeer sinews from pegs in the walls.

There was one fire to every four compart-ments, and Pocohontas sometimes stopped to kick a glowing log which had fallen from the hearth-stone, or bent to pick up a fir cone and drop it into the embers. Her father and the braves were seated round the central fire. They made room for her on their buffalo robes, and she warmed her hands, inhaling the tobacco smoke with quick little sniffs and listening to the conversation.

It seemed that trouble was afoot. Wabun-sonacook was frowning and talking of certain pale-faced men who had come from the sea and built themselves a village not far from K'tchi-sipik, the Great Water. They had weapons which spoke like thunder and could kill a man without appearing to touch him, and their great white chief grew a bush of hair on his face and was for ever suing the Redskins for corn. The braves grunted. Their squaws had gathered the harvest and stored the grain. There was only enough for Werowocomoco, yet they had heard from other tribes that the Palefaces paid well. They had seen beads and hatchets and a strange hard substance like ice in which a man could see his own face more clearly than in the river. The Redskins desired these things, but they needed their own corn, and they were not sure that the Palefaces with their thunder-sticks had come in peace.

Pocohontas listened without speaking. She had been through the forest, hoping to meet one of the white strangers, and had returned disappointed, but she did not say so. Her father would have smiled indulgently, for she was the apple of his eye, but some of the squaws were awake and such a confession might have made them envious. They worked very hard and were inclined to think that Pocohontas was spoiled because she sometimes slipped away and joined her brothers instead of helping to till the fields, mend the wigwams or prepare the furs. They would certainly have grumbled if they had heard of her escapade, so she contented herself with saying, "I wish I could see the great white chief," and playfully wrestled with her brother when he made some laughing suggestion about a future husband.

That night Pocohontas found it difficult to sleep. She lay on a buffalo robe, and with eyes half-closed watched the embers of the fire burning low and listened to the sounds which came through the open doorway. She heard the rustle of pine and birch as they whispered together, the chuckle of a little brook which rippled over the pebbles, the croaking of the tree frogs and the distant call of a bird to its mate. Suddenly she sat up. Someone was stirring. Her father had risen and there was a sound of footsteps and low voices at the doorway. She wriggled on knees and elbows and peered round the edge of the wooden partition which separated her from her neighbours.

Her father was seated before a dying fire not far from the doorway, and before him stood a Powhatan from another village. Pocohontas could see that he had come very fast because his leggings were torn, beads of perspiration stood on his forehead, and his chest rose and fell under his bearskin cloak. He was talking in quick eager whispers, but Pocohontas, whose ear was trained to catch the smallest rustle among the forest leaves, heard every word. And as she listened, her lips parted and her eyes gleamed.

She drew a deep breath. So they had cap-

tured the great white chief. Opechancanough,
a Redskin warrior, with two hundred braves had

POWHATAN *Appamatuck*
*Held this state & fashion when Capt. Smith
was deliuered to him prisoner
1607*

surrounded him when he had left his boat in the
river and was wandering in the forest. He must
have made friends with some of the Powhatans

in distant villages, for one of them was acting as his guide; when the braves had levelled their bows to shoot, the cunning Paleface had seized the Redskin and used his body as a shield and, of course, they could not kill their brother. Then the great white chief had run, but he had sunk in a quagmire and so the braves had seized him and, with their loud war-cries and slow circling dances, had led him into captivity.

Pocohontas stole nearer. A look of anxiety crept into her eyes and she clenched her fists. If the white man had been killed before she had seen him, she would send her brothers for Opechancanough's scalp. She listened. The messenger was growing more excited. The great white chief was alive. He had given Opechancanough a magic disc in which a tiny trembling needle would show him which way to turn if he were lost, so the Redskin had spared his life but kept him in captivity, carrying him from village to village for all the braves to see. He had travelled many miles through plain and forest, up the Rappahannock and Potomac rivers and now, at last, he was on his way to Werowocomoco that Wabunsonacook, the greatest of all the Powhatans, might decide his fate.

Pocohontas stole softly back to her buffalo robe, curled herself up like a little cat, and went to sleep with a smile of satisfaction on her lips and the determination to rise before the other squaws and go with the braves to meet the captive.

But Pocohontas was young. Her day in the forest had tired her, eavesdropping by night had kept her awake very late, so she slept like a healthy little animal and was startled next morning by the sound of a drum, the shrill discordant yells which she knew so well and the padding of feet, taking two steps forward and one back, in a native war-dance.

Kicking the buffalo robe into a corner, she pushed her bare toes into her moccasins and sped, like a deer, to the door of the wigwam.

Outside, the braves, in all the glory of war-paint and feathers, were waving tomahawks above their heads, posturing, grunting and shouting Powhatan songs of triumph. Behind walked the captive with a Red Indian on each side. Under the broad brows his eyes looked keen and kindly. Pocohontas watched him. She was sure he was quick-witted and that his direct glance missed nothing. He was a fighter, too, and one who would seek adventure, perhaps a mighty hunter. She did not know, but she liked the strange, pale face which looked so composed and unafraid, the untidy beard, grey-brown like the pelt of a chipmunk, and the torn clothes so unlike anything that she had ever seen. Indeed, he was so strangely dressed that the squaws stared at him open-mouthed. Some of them giggled, then burst into shrill uncontrollable laughter, till the scowls and sharp commands of their husbands sent them waddling back to the wigwams to prepare a feast. They were out of sight, but for some time the sizzling of fat and the bubbling of water mingled with little splutters of laughter.

Pocohontas, who should have been helping to stew deers' meat in the big sun-baked cauldrons, neglected her duties and slipping past the busy squaws, ran to the doorway of the Council Chamber and peeped inside. On a wooden platform covered with matting sat her father, with a soft leather skirt round his waist and a triple necklace of wooden beads. He was wearing a beautiful head-dress of eagles' feathers and he held in his hand a pipe as long as his arm. On both sides of the Council Chamber sat the two hundred braves of Werowocomoco, each on a mat made of reeds with a coloured border, and in the middle a fire was burning. The logs crackled and with each puff of wind, which came through the open doorway, the smoke eddied to and fro, floating about in grey clouds until it passed through a hole in the roof. The prisoner, standing before Wabunsonacook, coughed and wiped his eyes, but otherwise seemed unperturbed. A mat was pulled near the fire and he sat upon it. Then the Chief of the Powhatans clapped his hands and the squaws came in with food.

Pocohontas smiled. Her father was evidently pleased with the Paleface, for the feast was the best which Werowocomoco could produce. There was hominy boiled in water, fish fried in animal fat, little yellow cakes of Indian corn, stewed herbs and tough pieces of meat which had been dried in the sun during the summer, then rolled up tightly and stored for the winter. The prisoner and the Redskins ate heartily and Wabunsonacook spoke courteously and kindly, as he did to every guest of the tribe. But when the feast was over and the squaws had carried away the platters and the scraps, a change came over the old, chief's face and he sternly demanded the reason of the white men's coming.

Pocohontas listened with bated breath as the captive talked. The Redskin, who had acted as his guide, seemed to understand him, for he nodded and smiled, explaining in Algonquin what the stranger was saying. Several times Pocohontas put her hand in front of her mouth to prevent herself from laughing. The Paleface was clever, but his eyes betrayed him. He was undoubtedly lying when he said that the weather had driven him to K'tchisipik. His pronunciation of K'tchisipik, too, nearly made Pocohontas lose her balance, for she was standing tiptoe. He called it Chesapeake and for some reason he often referred to the Powhatan River as the James.

The little girl's eyes twinkled. The white man told a tale almost as well as a Redskin, and he was amusing to watch. He stood so still and never moved his hands except to stroke his beard. She hoped that her father would adopt him into the tribe and then perhaps he would make clothes for her like his own. She looked at Wabunsonacook and tried to read his expression. He was frowning and speaking with slow deliberation. Then he paused and gave an order. Three of the Redskins leapt to their feet, rolled two great stones before the fire and began to beat a fierce tattoo upon a drum. For a minute the captive looked startled and then he shrugged, as somebody seized him, forced him to his knees and held his head on the stones. With a blood-curdling yell, two gigantic braves, bedaubed with paint and decked with birds' feathers, raised their clubs and were about to beat out his brains, when they were startled by a low snarl of rage at their feet. They paused with their clubs in mid-air. There, on her knees, with her head on the prisoner's, lay Pocohontas, snarling and glowering like an angry tigress.

"Wa, wa! Mataoka—*pocohontas*," cried the Redskins, who had not even seen her come in. Their eyes glowed like embers and they turned away, some in sullen anger, some with a grunt of disgust. They had thought that all the squaws were busy in the wigwams, and now the chief's daughter had unexpectedly exercised the right of every Indian woman to spare a captive's life and claim him as her own property.

Pocohontas looked at her father. He made no comment but a gesture of dismissal. The Redskins rolled away the two stones and left the Council Chamber, grimacing and shrugging. The white man shook hands with Pocohontas, who laughed delightedly at so unfamiliar an action and led the way to her father's wigwam, while all the other squaws peeped round the doors chattering like startled jays.

The little girl spread the best buffalo robe before the fire, filled a long-handled pipe with choicest tobacco and offered it to the Paleface, and while he puffed till his cheeks were red, she lit it with a glowing cinder, dexterously held between two sticks. Then she talked, sitting back on her heels and chirruping like a small wise bird with her head on one side. When he made no answer, but smoked and smiled by turns, she fell to staring, touching the buttons on his coat, puzzled at the nature of the animal from whose bones they were made, fingering the puffy breeches and silk garters, laughing at the dirty white collar and diving into the pockets, which were as rich in treasure as a magic wallet. The coins astonished her.

"His Majesty King James I," said the Paleface, pointing to the crowned head on the coin,

King Powhatan *comands C Smith to be flayne, his daughter Pokahontas beggs his life, his thankfullnefs and how he Subiecled 39 of their kings reade, & hiftory*

Pocohontas begs Captain John Smith's life

but all the respect which Pocohontas showed
was to lick it and make a grimace.

The Paleface with the help of his Powhatan guide taught her much. She learned that the men of his race knew him as Captain John Smith, but her tongue seemed to twist when she tried to say it, so she used her own language and called him Cau-cu-rouse (the great leader). He told her that he had made a village on the banks of the river, calling it Jamestown, after his great white King who lived across the water. If the little Indian princess would coax her father to let him return, she could visit Jamestown and feast with all the Palefaces. There were presents for her, hatchets which were not made of stone but of a hard sharp metal which she had never seen. There were beads bright as the rainbow, or yellow as the golden rod which grew in her own woods in the summer. There were little mirrors in which she could see her face, and bells which she could hang round her neck so that when she ran or danced she would make music. He took her hand and rubbed it against his sleeve. There was cloth like that—scarlet, blue and green—for any brave or squaw in Werowocomoco who would bring corn to the Palefaces.

Pocohontas bit her knuckles and thought deeply. She had saved Caucurouse's life, so he was her property and she might do as she liked with him. For a long time she was silent, then she sprang up and sought her father.

The result was that two days later, Captain John Smith returned to Jamestown with twelve young Powhatans, who were to bring back two guns and a grindstone to Werowocomoco.

Of course, such an adventure as this was bound to bring changes into the life of the little Red Indian girl. Hunting in the forests with her brothers or helping the squaws in all the domestic work of the village now seemed very dull to Pocohontas, and she was never so happy as when she stood within sight of the triangular fort and the great guns which guarded Caucurouse's village.

She often visited Jamestown and became a great favourite among the settlers, for she could coax her father and the braves to bring them corn. Sometimes she led her own people to the edge of the fort and held a fair, where the white men could exchange their kettles and gewgaws for soft deerskin robes, bushels of maize, turkeys, squirrels and the fragrant tobacco on which they were growing as dependent as the Indians.

But although his daughter loved her new friends, the Great Powhatan, as the Englishmen called Wabunsonacook, feared and distrusted them. He hated these pale interlopers who paddled up the rivers and set their great wooden crosses on the islands. They wanted to see each nook and cranny in valley, hill and forest. They were haughty and meddlesome, ever ready to ask for corn but never willing to give more than a trumpery toy when the Redskins desired their swords and magic firearms. So the Great Powhatan planned thefts and ambushes and unexpected attacks on the settlement; but whenever she could, Pocohontas slipped away from Werowocomoco, stole through the forest and warned Caucurouse.

She must have saved many lives, yet for all her kindness she was still a tomboy, and some years later when one of the settlers was writing about Jamestown, he described how "Powhatan's daughter, sometimes resorting to our fort, did get the boys forth with her into the market-place and make them wheel, falling on their hands, turning their heels upward, whom she would follow and wheel so herself all the fort over."

But even a tomboy grows up, and a day came when Mataoka, the *pocohontas*, was christened Rebecca by an English priest, and married to an English gentleman who had laughed at her somersaults but loved her kind heart. His name was John Rolfe, and perhaps his little Red Indian wife told him how comfort had been brought to the Redskins by a certain great spirit and his burning hair, for Master Rolfe was the first Englishman to plant tobacco and sow the seed of wealth in Virginia.

CHAPTER VII

MARTIN ON THE ISLE OF DEVILS

[A.D. 1609. Sir George Somers reaches the Bermudas]

Somebody was moaning "The Lord have mercy on us! The Lord have mercy on us!" in a low monotonous chant, and the terrified sobs of two women, huddled in a corner of the cabin, mingled with the roaring of the sea and the wind.

A wave, like a vast cloud, broke over poop and quarter-deck, covering the ship with a torrent of rushing water, which carried the helmsman from the helm and wrested the whip-staff from his hand so that it whirled from side to side. The admiral was below at the capstan, encouraging the men and giving out "comforting waters" to hearten their spirits and warm their bodies, but the shock sent him sprawling on his face. It felled most people, and the wail "We drown! We drown!" shrilled above the sound of wind and waves and so unmanned the seamen that they waded towards the spar-deck as though through a flood, shouting, "Let us die above the hatches in the free air."

Nobody knew what had happened to the other ships in the squadron. Nine of them, including a ketch and a pinnace, had left England, proud of belonging to the *London Virginia Company*, which was sending five hundred colonists to the New World, where a certain Captain John Smith had built a fort, called Jamestown. They were beautiful ships, some of them old-fashioned with a castle fore and aft, but most of them lying low on the water, with long slim hulls, sails square-rigged and their upper works consisting of a fo'c'sle and quarter-deck with a poop at the stern. There was the *Blessing* which carried a score of women and children and a crew of hardy seamen, eager to get a glimpse of Virginia, the *Unity* with seventy landsmen besides her master and his mariners, the *Diamond* which was the flagship of the vice-admiral, the *Lion*, the *Swallow* and the *Sea-Venture*. They had sailed from England in June with instructions to leave the Canaries a hundred leagues to the eastward and to "steere away directly for Virginia without touching at the West Indies." All went merrily until they were in the neighbourhood of the Bahamas, when the tail of a hurricane caught and scattered them, and for days the little *Sea-Venture* battled alone with wind and waves.

When the worst of the storm was over, it was found that the ship had sprung a leak and, although three pumps were at work night and day, the water continued to rise in the hold. It was then that Martin came to his senses. When he had first stood on board and seen nothing but water all round him, and the coast of England a mere blue thread in the distance, he had been frightened, and in spite of his eleven years, had clung to his father's arm, for he was country-bred and had never before set eyes on the sea. The other boys had sniggered, calling him "land-lubber" and "country-mouse," and once, when he had fallen asleep on deck after being very sea-sick, he awoke to find himself tied to the lower part of a mast by a woman's apron and all the children, little girls included, dancing round him shouting, "Look at Martin's leading-strings!" One of them tried to feed him with pap made from a ship's biscuit soaked in salt water, and Martin was so ashamed and disgusted that he burst the apron-strings and never again showed any fear of the sea, although he had many an inward qualm.

At first the fury of the storm had terrified him, but he bit his lips and pretended not to mind it, sitting with his arms round the neck of Duke, his dog, which licked his face and whined whenever a loud crash above showed that a wave had swept over the ship. The children, who had mocked him in calm weather, were now pale and frightened. Some of them burst into tears when they learned about the leak, but Martin was suddenly galvanized into action. He heard the order "All hands to the bails!"

and seizing a small wooden pail in which his mother had packed cheese for the voyage, he climbed after the seamen into the hold.

For a long time he stood on the ballast and bailed, while the water seemed to be rising steadily. Many of the landsmen were helping. Some were naked, with their long cloth hose untrussed and the points hanging down over their knees. Some, like the mariners, had stripped to the waist and were drawing in their breath with little, sharp whistles as the salt water made their bodies tingle. Others were fully clothed, the richer ones looking strangely bedraggled, for the colours in their soaked doublets were running and the stuffing in their bombasted breeches was so clogged with water that it smelt of wet hay. They had seized every vessel on which they could lay hands and were bailing feverishly. Kettles, pails, cauldrons and barricoes were all in use, and Martin noticed that two of the most important officials on board, Sir Thomas Gates and Captain Newport, were taking their turn at the pumps.

As the hours passed he began to grow tired, and when his limbs became so stiff that he could not move somebody handed him to one of the seamen, and took his place, while he dozed below decks with his head on a coil of rope and the dog licking his hands.

For three days and three nights the men

bailed, and Martin with his wooden pail waded among them, putting biscuit and chunks of cheese into their mouths, fetching the wine

Sir George Somers

which some of them had stowed in their sea-chests and listening as they pledged one another, each time taking "a last farewell." Whenever he came up, with the dog picking its way along the slippery deck behind him, he saw the admiral, Sir George Somers, sitting on the poop, trying to ride the ship on an even keel. His face was haggard for want of sleep and food, and his eyes had sunk far back in his head, but Martin never heard him utter a complaint. He whistled cheerily to the men, calling words of encouragement and urging them to pump and bail, for the water was still rising and many of the mariners were so spent with fasting and work that they were falling asleep where they stood.

It was Martin who heard the faint cry "Land ahoy!" At first, he could not believe his ears, but when he saw the admiral put both hands, cupwise, round his mouth and shout again, he ran cheering towards the hold, yelling, "Land, land, land!" and leaping so madly that the dog thought he was playing a game, seized him by the seat of his breeches, and growled with sheer joy, shaking its head so violently from side to side, that the breeches were torn and a long wisp of bombast hung down behind, making Martin look as though he had a tail.

"Land!" he screamed again and "La-and" echoed the deep voice of the admiral from the poop.

The fainting men gave the ghost of a cheer and gathering together their strength bailed with as much energy as they could muster. The women came up from the cabin, their pale faces bright with smiles, and even Martin's mother, though scandalised at the sight of her son's breeches, stopped for a minute to shade her eyes with her hands and gaze at the distant coast, before hustling the boy below decks to her needles and thread.

Martin was somewhat annoyed at being treated in this summary manner. Since most of the men who were bailing had long ago stripped off their clothes, he did not understand why a hole in the back of his breeches should seem so disgraceful. He unlaced his points sulkily and sat in his doublet and cloth hose, hoping that his mother would not examine the tail of his shirt, where the marks of the dog's teeth were plainly visible. He was grumbling below his breath and twisting his fingers in and out of his woollen garters when the ship seemed to heel over, right herself and come to a sudden standstill. A long-drawn rasping sound was followed by a loud cry. The *Sea-Venture* shuddered. Something scraped near her keel and suddenly she began to sway and bump as though invisible hands were tossing her in the air and letting her fall roughly on to some hard, uneven surface. Martin leapt to his feet and sped breechless to the hatches with the tail of his shirt flapping.

A scene of confusion met his eyes. Some of

the seamen were helping the women and children up to the quarter-deck. Others were hauling on the ropes, shouting to one another and battling with the sails against the wind. Landsmen and ship's boys were at the pumps and bails, Sir George Somers, still on the poop, was giving orders, quietly and with white lips, while Duke sat at his feet with ears cocked and tongue out, panting and beating his tail with rhythmic thuds against the deck.

The *Sea-Venture* had struck a coral reef and was bumping from rock to rock.

Martin's head swam. The waves which were dashing against the ship's sides looked angry and the spray flipped in his face, making his eyes smart until they filled with tears. There was something sinister and cruel in the green water which coiled round the rocks and rose steadily higher and higher in the hold. But the two crags ahead were yet more ominous. Martin shut his eyes. He did not want to see the gallant little *Sea-Venture* dashed to pieces and he wondered vaguely how long it would take to drown and whether Duke could swim. He shivered a little and wished that people would stop shouting, but the more irritable he became the louder they cried and a tremendous jerk brought a chorus of "Jesu!" "Heaven help us!"

With a half-stifled sob, Martin opened his eyes and found that the *Sea-Venture* was wedged upright between the two rocks with nine feet of water in her hold, the mariners ruefully scratching the backs of their heads and Sir George Somers gazing into the distance.

Scarcely half a mile away lay an island in a white ring of foam. Slender trees tapered towards the sky. Cedars spread dark branches among the silver leaves of the wild olive, and here and there a gleam of scarlet or yellow flashed from the undergrowth. With the skimming clouds above and the glitter of green water below, it looked like an enchanted isle which had risen from the sea at the touch of a magic wand.

Martin, forgetting his fright, ran to the side of the ship crying, "It's fairyland!" But the mariners were pale. One of them shuddered and crossed himself. "Fairyland!" he muttered. "'Tis Bermuda, which men call the Isle of Devils." Then all the stories which the seamen had told him, when he had been so frightened at the beginning of the voyage, came crowding into Martin's mind. He remembered tales of an island where demons hid among the trees and beautiful girls had the bodies of monsters and fed upon shipwrecked mariners. Was this lovely land, which looked like a haven of peace, the famous Isle of Devils dreaded and avoided by every mariner?

With wide terrified eyes, Martin stared across

the sea, and as he was looking, isle and water changed colour, growing from a soft, dull green to a luminous jade with the dark tones of the cedars like deep shadows against the clouds, and the encircling foam as bright as dewdrops on a May morning. He gazed, waiting nervously for a demon face to peer at him through the branches, when someone smote him violently on the shoulder, and a voice crying, "Now then Martin Lack-Breeches, it's time you were dressed and in the boat!" reminded him of his unconventional attire. Grabbing at his hose, he ran to find his mother and saw the ship's boat, freighted with men, women and children, being rowed towards the Isle of Devils.

When Martin himself was in the boat, he soon forgot about the demons, for down in the clear depths of the water he could see the fish swimming among the coral branches. They glowed like small, coloured lamps, and were almost as fantastic in shape as the dragons on the painted cloths which fashionable people hung upon their walls in England. Martin watched them, fascinated, until the boat reached the shallows and her keel scraped in the sand.

The island itself was as beautiful as the sea which surrounded it. The air was soft and a little breeze just stirred the grass. Wild duck and mallard swam in the shallow pools, and in the distance Martin could hear the faint "Peea-weet" of plovers disturbed by the unwonted noise.

With his hand on Duke's neck, the boy walked through the woods, picking wild mulberries and whistling to the white herons which were so tame that they settled at his feet and showed no fear of the dog. The beauty of the trees and flowering shrubs, and the green grass starred with blossoms filled Martin with rapture, and as he passed from the woods into a little glade, he laughed, saying, "This is no isle of Devils, is it, Duke? This is—." But he did not finish his sentence, and when he looked at the dog, his heart almost stopped beating.

Duke scented danger. He was sniffing the ground, uttering short, sharp whines. His ears were cocked, his hindquarters trembling and the rough hair round his neck standing on end like bristles. Martin looked round. He saw no one, but the beauty of the island had suddenly grown oppressive, and for the first time he noticed the witch-like cactus hedges with their prickly pears and fat, fleshy leaves like hairy hands. He peered furtively through the branches wishing that the fruit and flowers had not lured him away from the others, and whispering nervously, "The Isle of Devils."

A scratching and squealing behind the cactus hedge made him cling in a frenzy of fear to Duke's collar. But the dog leaped away from him and, terrified, he looked to right and to left, not knowing which way to turn. He wanted to run, but his legs were like lead and the noise was coming nearer. Martin could hear the sounds of heavy snorting breath and the beating of cloven hoofs upon the ground. Shrieking "The devils! The devils!" he tore himself from the spot just as a herd of wild pigs, grunting and squealing, dashed helter-skelter through the glade with Duke at their heels.

Martin sat on the grass to recover his breath. He felt very much ashamed and was thankful that no one had been there to see the ignominious cause of his fright. When he felt better he strolled back to the shore, trying to look as unconcerned as possible, and announced that the island could furnish sufficient pork to feed an army. One of the boys innocently shouted "Hurrah for devilled trotters!" and could not understand why Martin blushed to the roots of his hair and glared at him.

Fortunately, the subject changed from pigs to fish and other things which would satisfy the hunger of the most fastidious castaway, for the island was rich in foodstuffs. There were red and white berries for dessert, fowls and eggs, fish so abundant that they could be caught in shallow water with the hands, turtles which gave oil as sweet as butter and were so large that one of them made a good meal for fifty-two men.

As time passed, Martin sometimes longed for a taste of dry bread, but all the flour and biscuits in the ship had been ruined by the salt water and the castaways could only eat what the island provided. It amused the boy to watch his mother frying fish in turtles' oil, roasting birds on a forked stick and making omelettes from the eggs which he found for her in the woods. In England, he had sometimes gabbled his grace before meals, without really thinking of what he was saying, but the words now held a new meaning for him, and he felt very humble and grateful as he stood bareheaded under the open sky reciting the old, familiar prayer:

O Lord which giv'st Thy creatures for our food,
Hearbs, beastes, birdes, fish and other giftes of Thine,
Blesse these Thy giftes that they may doe us good;
And we may live to praise Thy name divine.
And when the time is come this life to end,
Vouchsafe our soules to Heaven may ascende.

For nine months Martin led a castaway's life, enjoying to the full the many tasks which fell to his lot. At first, he had to collect branches to make the wattled sleeping huts and gather reeds and mosses to thatch their roofs. He had to help the mariners, too, for the *Sea-Venture* was still wedged between the rocks and there was baggage and cargo to be salved. Martin knew that this was important, for Captain John Smith had sent a list of articles which he considered indispensable for a colonist's personal outfit. Martin could remember some of the things and the prices which his father had paid for them:

	s.	d.		s.	d.
A Monmouth cap ...	1	10	Seven ells of canvase to		
Three shirts	7	6	make a bed & bolster		
One Wastecoat ...	2	2	to be filled in Virginia,		
One suit of canvas ...	7	6	serving for two men		
One suit of Frize ...	10	0			
One suit of Cloth ...	15	0	Five ells of coarse can-		
Three pairs of Irish			vase to make a bed ...	5	0
stockings	4	0			
Four pairs of shoes ...	8	8	One coarse rug to be		
One pair of garters ...	0	10	used at sea for two		
One dozen of points ...	8	0	men		
One pair of canvas					
sheets	8	0			

Fortunately, most of the colonists were able to save their goods, but the salt water had stained all Martin's canvas and spoiled two pairs of shoes, so that he felt rather rueful when he examined his baggage. He had, however, little time to lament, for personal effects were not the only things which had to be salved. Sir George Somers was determined to build two new pinnaces that he might carry out the orders of the *London Virginia Company* and take the colonists to the New World. This meant that sails, guns and tackle had to be salved from the *Sea-Venture*, and Martin spent many an hour holding a sack while the seamen pulled out nails and stripped off the iron-work.

The building of the new ships was a source of great interest to the boy, who loved to help the carpenter plane the cedar wood and straighten the old nails. He was proud of belonging to a company of men who did not despair when they could find neither pitch nor tar, but used instead some wax, washed ashore from a wreck, and a sort of lime which they made from pounded stones mixed with water. When the ships were ready and named the *Deliverance* and the *Patience*, there was the task of finding provisions, and although Martin always felt a little embarrassed when he saw a pig, he thoroughly enjoyed his foraging expeditions with Duke, who proved an invaluable hunter, and he gladly helped his mother to powder and salt the pork or preserve it in turtles' oil.

The castaway's life seemed to him ideal, and when at last the two ships put to sea, he stood on deck sorrowfully watching the Isle of Devils until he could not distinguish it from the blue sky above or the green water below. The other boys called him " Martin Sulky-Face," because he spent his time staring dreamily into the distance instead of playing at quoits with them. But Martin took no notice. He was thinking "The admiral has left the English flag on the Isle of Devils. One day I shall go back and salute it."

And that was a dream which came true, for

six years later, when Martin was a tall lad of seventeen, he sailed away from Virginia and became an apprentice to the Somers Company, which the English merchants formed to colonise the Isle of Devils and develop trade between the Bermudas and the New World. The young apprentice was something of a joke among his fellow-colonists, for he never stirred abroad without a sleepy old dog called Duke, and for some reason or other, he always looked sheepish when he met a herd of wild pigs. All his life the island still kept for him some of the enchantment of his first sight of it, when it seemed a fairy land, and many years later he read a poem by a certain Andrew Marvell, which seemed to him to say all the things that he felt about it:

> Where the remote Bermudas ride
> In the ocean's bosom unespied,
> From a small boat that row'd along
> The listening woods received this song:
>   "What should we do but sing His praise
> That led us through the watery maze
> Unto an isle so long unknown,
> And yet far kinder than our own?
> Where He the huge sea-monsters wracks,
> That lift the deep upon their backs,
> He lands us on a grassy stage,
> Safe from the storms' and prelates' rage:
> He gave us this eternal Spring
> Which here enamels everything,

And sends the fowls to us in care
On daily visits through the air:
He hangs in shades the orange bright
Like golden lamps in a green night,
And does in the pomegranates close
Jewels more rich than Ormuz shows:
He makes the figs our mouths to meet
And throws the melons at our feet;
But apples plants of such a price,
No tree could ever bear them twice.
With cedars chosen by His hand
From Lebanon He stores the land;
And makes the hollow seas that roar
Proclaim the ambergris on shore.
He cast (of which we rather boast)
The Gospel's pearl upon our coast;
And in these rocks for us did frame
A temple where to sound His name.
O, let our voice His praise exalt
Till it arrive at Heaven's vault,
Which then (perhaps) rebounding may
Echo beyond the Mexique bay!"

Thus sung they in the English boat
A holy and a cheerful note:
And all the way, to guide their chime,
With falling oars they kept the time.

CHAPTER VIII

NICK AND THE MUTINEERS

[A.D. 1610. Henry Hudson's last voyage]

James Bay was a waste of snow-covered ice, sometimes lying smooth and flat, sometimes rising into low hillocks, but everywhere drearily white. Close to the shore the *Discovery* was aground, a ghost-ship frozen in, with the white snow on her decks and her masts pointing to the sky like the bony arms of a skeleton. All around her, snow-capped rocks rose from the frozen mud-flats, and here and there the half-buried stump of a tree made a jagged grey streak in the monotonous landscape. No sound broke the silence. There was not a breath of wind and the branches of spruce and juniper, bending beneath the weight of the snow, were motionless.

As silently as the gaunt timber wolves which slunk through the forest, Jack Hudson and Nicholas Syms moved from tree to tree, gathering fallen twigs and fir cones. Their eyes were dull and furtive. The skin was drawn tightly over their cheekbones and their bloodless lips hid gums which were blackened by scurvy.

"I'm hungry," whispered Nick. The hoarse notes seemed to hang in the air like something solid, and two tears oozed from the corners of his eyes and rolled to his lips. He licked them away lest they should freeze. "I'm hungry," he whimpered, and he grasped Jack's shoulder with a lean mittened hand and tried to shake him, but he had not the strength.

Jack smiled wanly. He was used to Nick's outbursts and he was hungry himself, so he understood. "Ptarmigan," he said, "as soon as we can make up the fire. Come along!" He stooped and tried to buckle his belt round his bundle of sticks, but his fingers were so cold and his fur gloves so clumsy that he could only twist it, and some of the twigs fell out as he toiled across the snow.

Nick followed with trembling lips and sagging knees. He was thinking of his home in Wapping and cursing the day when he had joined the *Discovery* as cabin-boy. He was thinking, too, of the terrible journey among the northern icefloes and the disloyal murmuring of the men who believed that the master had lost his way. He stumbled, and the fir cones began to roll along the hard surface of the snow, till he nearly cried with rage and weakness.

"The north-west passage!" he muttered, grabbing feebly at the fallen booty, "pah! A wild goose chase." And because "wild goose" reminded him of sage and onions and a bellyful of victuals, the tears started to his eyes and he staggered blindly after Jack, relieved at last to reach the shed which served as winter-quarters.

It was a log cabin with a small hole in the roof, from which the smoke rose in a straight grey line against the windless sky. The sloping roof was white with snow which stood nearly a foot high, and long blue icicles hung from the eaves. A path had been swept clear at the door, but the snow had drifted so high against the walls that the hut looked almost too small for human habitation.

Jack and Nick pushed the door open and went in. A wood fire was burning on a roughly fashioned stone hearth and the men were sitting round it. They made a strange group in the fire-light, for their bodies were so wrapped about with blankets that they looked shapeless, their beards and hair were matted, and their eyes so dulled by hunger that they gave no life to the haggard faces.

They were all there—able seamen, gunner, cooper and carpenter, Edward Wilson, the twenty-two-year-old surgeon, Wydowse, the young mathematician with the querulous voice and peevish manners, and John King, the quarter-master, staunch and loyal in every difficulty. There was Greene, the ne'er-do-well, who had come on board at the last minute. He had started full of friendship for the master, but had quarrelled with him and was now scarcely on speaking terms. He was holding a basin while the surgeon was bandaging the boatswain's feet, from which the nails had been frozen. Whenever the patient moaned, Abacuk Prickett, the landsman, whom Nick disliked for his silky manners, read aloud from the Bible and licked his lips.

They were crouching round the fire, twenty hungry men and Henry Hudson, the master.

When the boys came in, Hudson had his long thin hands stretched towards the blazing logs. He was joking about the ptarmigans, which Mathues, the cook, was plucking. Nick glowered and tightened his belt, but Jack cast a wistful look at his father. The men were taking the joke in ill part. Old Juet, who had once been mate, nourished a grievance against Hudson for punishing his disloyal grumbling by degrading him and putting Bylot in his place. He glared at Hudson, muttering under his breath, "There's enough cheese and biscuits for those who have the key. We found *that* out on the voyage."

Nick took a furtive look at Jack, whose hands were clenched, but the master, without turning his head, suggested that his men might not wish to starve on the return journey, and Abacuk Prickett fluttered the pages of his Bible, looking for the story of the wise and the foolish virgins.

Ptarmigan soup was a diversion, but Nick was still miserably hungry and he went to sleep,

dreaming of food and waking with a start whenever somebody groaned with the pain of a frost-
bitten foot.

Night after night he twisted and tossed on
the narrow shelf which was his bed, sometimes
dozing fitfully, sometimes lying awake listening
to the whispers of others who were as sleepless
as himself. Often he woke to find Greene and
Juet huddled over the fire snarling like two
angry dogs deprived of their bones, and he
heard them accuse the master of feeding himself while others starved. He watched their
narrow bloodshot eyes staring resentfully at
Hudson who slept with his cloak over his head.
Then he turned softly on his side to peer over
the edge of his bunk at Jack, who was lying
below. He always saw the same pale face,
watchful and listening, with sunken eyes wide
open. Sometimes he was too tired to do anything but smile, otherwise he let his arm hang
down and snapped his fingers. Then a thin
cold hand would grasp his tightly and he knew
that the master's son felt that the cabin-boy was
a friend, in spite of his bad temper.

For seven long months, life brought scarcely
any change. Day after day, Nick trudged
drearily through the snow, helping Jack to
gather firewood or straining his eyes in the hope
of seeing a ptarmigan, whose winter plumage
was scarcely visible against the white back-

ground. He longed for Spring, but cursed it when it came, for with the warmer weather the ptarmigan disappeared, and the men, weakened by scurvy and starvation, had lost their skill with the musket and seldom brought down the wild duck which passed overhead on their way to other climes.

Like a grey shadow Nick passed from wood to valley and hill, seeking food. He scraped away the snow and gathered mosses which Mathues cooked, and when the ice began to melt he found some frogs, which he shared with Jack. Once a wandering Cree appeared like a goblin in the forest. He was frightened of the white men, but Hudson cajoled him to the camp and gave him a knife, some buttons and a looking-glass, and his delighted grin of surprise made Nick laugh for the first time in six months. The laugh was followed by the warm comfort of a good meal, for the Cree returned next day drawing a sledge behind him. On it he had placed two deerskins, two beaverskins and a large hunk of meat.

Everyone stood round the fire while Mathues cooked, inhaling the exquisite odour of roast venison, fingering the knives at their belts, impatient for the feast.

"We'll get meat, now," thought Nick, "for he's sure to come again to barter for trifles."

But the Cree went away. He never came back

and the men grumbled that Hudson had mal-
treated him, refusing to give a hatchet for one
deerskin but demanding two. Greene and Juet
muttered angrily. "He'd starve every other
man," they said, "to satisfy his own greed,"
and when he thought of the meat, Nick, too,
felt resentful, but he avoided looking at Jack,
whose watchful eyes were glancing from face to
face.

The appearance of the Cree was a prelude to
warmer weather and soon the men were able to
grub in the ground for roots and, as the ice
melted, to go fishing. Yet the small addition to
their rations did not make life easier, and never
a day passed without black looks and muttered
oaths. Those men who were still strong enough
to give vent to their feelings were rapidly becoming mutinous. Only Philip Staffe, the carpenter, and John King, the boatswain, shrugged
their shoulders, accepting their lot and murmuring, "Have done! Have done!" when Juet
and Greene sat over the fire and whispered.
The sick, moaning with pain and hunger, were
too weak either to talk or to listen. Jack Hudson
was silent and watchful but his hands twitched
nervously, and Nick scarcely knew what to do
or think, for he was torn between his affection
for the son and his resentment against the
father.

He was glad when James Bay was at last free

from ice, for this turned his thoughts in another direction, and he worked hard helping the crew to clean and repair the *Discovery* and to take in

Hudson Bay

water, wood and ballast. The change of occupation and the thought of the voyage home made him light-hearted, and he hummed cheerily, thinking of Wapping and all the good meals which he would eat under his mother's roof. He did surreptitious kindnesses to the sick, and when the others railed at them, trying to rouse them from their stupor and make them work, he would have taken their part if he had not been afraid.

Now that hope was high and there was work to be done, time seemed to pass more quickly and, before long, Nick found himself standing on the deck of the *Discovery*, shading his eyes with his hand, while the details of the landscape grew dimmer and dimmer, and the log cabin, which had been his home for the last eight months, was scarcely distinguishable from the trees behind it.

Nick was happy. "Wapping," he whispered and he hugged himself, grinning. With his blackened gums and yellow skin, he looked as grotesque as a painted gargoyle, and Juet, who was passing, pushed him against the woodwork. "Wapping?" he sneered. "Home? You fool! The master's still seeking the passage."

Nick's jaw dropped. He gave a little inarticulate cry and stumbled along the deck. "What?" he cried. "Wh—what did you say? I—"

"The master is not going home. He still seeks the north-west passage." Juet's voice rose higher and higher in his anger. "A fool's journey, when half the crew is sick. But *wait*." He shook his fist in the terrified boy's face and Nick edged for safety towards some of the others who were talking in a group. He was trembling and on the verge of tears. The disappointment had been too cruel.

Through a mist he saw the men gesticulating. He heard someone say that Hudson had deposed Bylot and made John King mate in his place. At this there was an angry roar and the men dispersed shouting: "Let the master and his ignorant mate carry the ship whithersoever they please!"

Nick went below. He shared a cabin amidships with Henry Greene, who stood gnawing his knuckles when the boy burst open the door and flung himself on the bunk. Jack Hudson passed and nodded kindly, but Nick was too miserable to return the greeting and, in any case, he seldom had the courage to acknowledge his friendship for Jack when Greene's eye was on him.

He lay with his hands behind his head trying to think, but he was so bitterly angry with Hudson that his mind seemed confused. He was still shaking and he longed for some food to steady his nerves. He was giddy, too, and his heart was beating so loudly that he could hear it in his own head. "Thud, thud, thud," it went, and "Food, food, food" echoed in his mind. Irresistibly his eye roved to the locker and stayed there. He knew that there was no bread. Before sailing Hudson had divided what remained. Nick remembered seeing the tears in his eyes when he gave each man his share. There was none of that left, but there was cheese—three-and-a-half pounds, the ration for seven days. Nick licked his lips. Then he slid off his bunk and crawled towards the locker. He did not care, now. He would eat all the cheese and die when there was no food left. Nothing mattered, now that he knew he was not going home. He struggled savagely with Greene who sat on the locker, but the habit of obedience was too strong. The voice of the master crying "Boy!" sent him snivelling to the door, and the usual round of tasks kept him from the locker till supper-time.

As the days passed, he grew busier, for he had to share the work of the sick men. Sometimes Jack came to help him, but Nick was always glad when he went away. The crew was so ill-disposed towards all whom Hudson held dear, that the boy was afraid of being seen with the master's son.

Long, hungry days were followed by dreary nights. Then came Saturday, June 23rd. Hudson had been steering north. The men had seen the ice and were afraid of it, and Nick went to bed early because *he* was afraid of them.

He slept while the *Discovery* was moored, and in his dreams he heard the floating blocks of ice knocking against the ship's sides and the plash of the water which followed. It was still night when he awoke and glanced sleepily at Greene's bunk. There was something unfamiliar about its tidiness. Nick sat up and rubbed his eyes. The bunk was empty. For a few seconds he wondered idly why Greene had not come to bed and wished he would hurry. In the day-time he liked to be alone in the cabin, but at night it was eerie. The thin partition rattled with each movement of the ship. All the woodwork seemed to squeak and groan, and the monotonous "tap-slush, tap-slush" against the sides of the vessel made him nervous. He stole to the door and looked out, but he could see no one and he shivered, hating the emptiness. He crept towards the kitchen, but Mathues, the cook, was not in his bunk. Only the crippled cooper lay in a corner groaning "Aah, my foot, my foot!" and taking no notice when a grey rat whisked across his bunk and sat with gleaming eyes on the locker.

Softly Nick crept to the gun-room where Juet slept. He thought that Greene might have joined his friend, but the gun-room was silent as a grave and Nick grew stiff with terror. Suddenly, he caught his breath. From the cabin next door came the murmur of voices, whispering, hissing. He pressed his ear to the partition and heard the low, hoarse muttering of angry men trying to speak softly. Then he tiptoed to the door. A knot in the wood had left a tiny hole, through which he peered with one eye. A candle, burning in a horn lantern, threw a pale, yellow light on the faces of some men. Nick thought that there were nine of them, but he could not see clearly. He recognised Juet, Greene and Mathues, and he heard some deprecating, sanctimonious phrases which he knew were from the lips of Abacuk Prickett. The remainder were out of his sight and their voices were so hoarse that he could not distinguish one from the other.

Greene seemed to be angry. He was standing upright. In his left hand he held a Bible, and with his right he tapped the cover impatiently. "I swear," he growled, "that I will do no man harm. What I do is for the good of the voyage and nothing else." He thrust the Bible into Juet's hand, and there was a note of triumph in the old man's voice as he took the same oath.

Outside, Nick's teeth were chattering. Through his tiny peep-hole the men with their emaciated cheeks and claw-like hands looked like evil spirits from another world and he watched them, fascinated, as they placed their hands on the Bible. There was no solemnity about the oath. The men seemed to be gloating over some secret which would bring them satisfaction. They looked at one another furtively, rubbing their hands and whispering. Nick strained his ears, but could not hear what they said till one spoke more loudly crying: "His rat of a son and all the sick men, too!" The snarling, "Aye, aye," which followed so scared the boy that he fled back to his empty cabin and lay quaking until Greene came to bed.

The night seemed terribly long and he was relieved when he heard the familiar sound of Mathues, the cook, carrying his kettle to the butts. Greene was sitting on the bunk listening with narrowed eyes, and Nick was startled by the sound of a scuffle, the excited voice of the surgeon shouting, "What has happened?" and the master's muffled answer, "They have bound me!"

Nick leapt to his feet, crying, "Jack!" but Greene's hand stifled the word on his lips, and Greene's knuckles in his throat and threats in his ears sent him whimpering and sore to the deck, waiting to carry out whatever orders might be given him.

He saw the shallop rocking at the *Discovery's* side, and the master, guarded by Mathues and a seaman, sitting there, in his "motley" coat with his wrists bound behind him. He heard bitter pleadings and angry retorts as one by one all the sick and the crippled were lowered into the shallop. Some were too weak to protest but Wydowse, the young mathematician, caught at Nick's sleeve as they hustled him to the rope-ladder and began to wail like a child.

"Take me back," he cried. "You shall have all my stuff if only you'll take me back." And when someone said, "You have been sick too long," he screamed till Nick pulled his cap over his ears to deaden the sound. He wanted to do something, but he was afraid and he stood by the rope-ladder biting his nails. The noise was terrible. The men were breaking up the hatches, looking for stores. The moaning of the sick in the shallop mingled with the shouting of the mutineers and the clash of swords where John King was fighting Juet near the hold. The old man was out-matched, but two able seamen came to his aid and soon John King was tossed into the shallop with little respect for life or limb.

Surging and pushing round the ladder, the men jostled until Nick was covered with bruises. He tried to elbow his way to a safer place and came upon Jack. The boy did not look like himself. There was no expression on his face. He was staring at the shallop while somebody held a musket at his head. He passed so close to Nick that their sleeves touched. Then without speaking he climbed over the ship's side, dropped with a thud at his father's feet and lay staring at the faces of the mutineers.

For an instant Nick caught his eye, but a sudden commotion made him turn. There, above the shallop stood the carpenter, Philip

Staffe. His musket and his carpenter's chest were on his shoulders and in his hand he held an iron pot half-full of meal. His eyes were burning and his bearded face was tense with indignation.

He faced the rebels. "Think you that an Ipswich carpenter will stay in the ship whose captain is cast adrift?" he cried. "I choose rather to commit myself to God's mercy, and for the love of the master to go down into the shallop, than stay with such villains."

He scrambled down and stood behind Hudson. "Who will follow?" he asked, looking up.

Nick began to cry. He took a step forward, blubbering like Wydowse, and Jack sat up suddenly with a light in his eyes. Nick saw him; saw, too, the one little pot of meal at the carpenter's side and wavered, for someone was shouting; "We've found it! We've found the food, which he has been hiding."

Nick's head swam. The word "food" was ringing in his ears and his eyes were fixed on the little iron pot in the shallop.

Greene's hand was on the rope-ladder. Juet was at the stern with a knife ready to cut the shallop free.

"Well?" sneered the mutineers.

Still staring at the pot of meal, Nick thrust out his hands with a gesture of terror. For a minute he hesitated, then he stepped back and with little feeble jerks began to haul up the rope-ladder.

Overhead the wild birds circled, screaming hoarsely. Below, the shallop rocked and a faintly mocking smile flickered across Jack Hudson's lips.

Hiccoughing and blubbering, Nick pulled with all his puny strength. Almost before he knew what had happened the ladder was in, the shallop cut from the stern and adrift, and the *Discovery* with her topsails up, heading for the open sea.

The cabin-boy was going home to Wapping, but he lay on his face crying, "Jack, Jack, Jack!" and, all through the nightmare voyage which followed, he never once thought of the cottage which he had loved so well.

He went about his tasks mechanically, gnawing his fingers and running when he passed Jack's cabin. As he nibbled the bread which the men had found among the stores, he thought of the shallop adrift with only a handful of meal. He had no pleasure in the sight of land, no interest in the winds and tides. When Greene and three of his companions were killed in a fight with some Esquimaux, he scarcely noticed their absence. One thought filled his mind, Jack haunted his dreams, slept with him by night and followed him by day. He could think of nothing else.

But there came a time when he was so weak, that every sense was numb and even Jack was forgotten. The extra bread had long since been consumed and soon the daily ration of half a bird and a cup of meal became a thing of the past. Nick was now too faint to dream or to think. He had barely enough energy to fry the bones of a bird in some candle grease, for his weekly allowance of food had dwindled to a pound of candles and a little vinegar.

Like gaunt wolves, he and his shipmates crawled about the deck on their stomachs, licking the planks and gnawing the hawsers. When old Juet died of starvation, they had scarcely the strength to push his body into the sea. Too weak to hoist and lower the sails, they sat, pale ghosts at the helm, steering their phantom ship towards Ireland. When the last candle was eaten, they stewed sea-weed and listened to the sound of the waves, for they had almost lost the power of speech.

Time meant nothing to them. They did not know that three months had passed since the shallop had been cast adrift. They scarcely recognised the coast of Galway when they sighted it, and wavered pitifully in their course as they followed a fishing boat which guided them into Bantry Bay.

Seated on deck with his head drooping and his mouth hanging open, Nick awaited his turn

Hudson's Last Voyage

to be rowed ashore for food. The Irish fisherman helped him into the boat, and taking pity
on him, gave him some bread and cheese and
a long drink of ale from a bottle. This unexpected meal brought him new strength. He sat
up and stared at the shore, his eyes feasting on
the green grass where the cattle grazed, and on
the little white houses where the people would
give him beer and beef.

As the boat's keel grated on the shingle, he
stood up, steadying himself by his hands. He
was smiling and whispering, when behind him
a flock of gulls rose in the air, wheeling and
screaming. Nick swayed as he stepped out of
the boat. Where had he heard that sound before? He thrust his fingers in his ears to shut
out the noise, but he could not hide the picture
which swam before his eyes.

With a cry, he flung his tattered cloak over
his head and ran stumbling and falling along
the beach. "I couldn't help it!" he sobbed,
"Oh, Jack, I couldn't help it!"

Overhead the sea-gulls followed for a little,
shrieking with wide-open beaks.

CHAPTER IX

MEG'S STORY

[A.D. 1618. The Execution of Sir Walter Ralegh]

"I can't tell you very much about him. You see, I saw him for the first and last time two weeks ago, and yet I feel as though a candle had been snuffed, and all of us left in the dark with just one little glow on the wick getting dimmer and dimmer.

"He was in prison before I was born, for treason they said, but everyone knew that it was a false charge, and his name was a household word. In our house, it was 'Sir Walter this' and 'Sir Walter that,' all day long, for he was my father's hero and we were for ever hearing tales of his daring against the Spaniards (plague take them!) and of all the efforts which he had made to plant a new England across the sea.

"Father used to talk about him when we were rowing past the Tower on our way to Westminster, and once he told me how the young prince had said, 'None but my father would keep such a bird in a cage.' Another time (I remember it quite clearly, though I can't have been more than five) we had a waterman who had sailed with Sir Walter to Guiana, long ago, in the days of Queen Bess. He shipped oars when he came to the Tower wharf and let the

The Tower of London
(*In the seventeenth century*)

boat drift as he gazed up at the barred windows.
'You can't see him now,' he said. 'There was
a time when he would stand up there, smiling,
and we crowded on to the wharf and shouted
to him. He used to take his exercise on the
ballium, up and down, up and down, like a
caged beast. But they've built a wall there
now, and we can't get a glimpse of him; and he,
well, he can't even see the river nor wave to the
mariners who pass.' I remember the old man's
face when he said it, and how he licked a tear
off his lips and rowed past the Tower so quickly
that the water splashed over the side of the
boat, and I began to whimper because I
thought I should be whipped for getting my
gown wet.

"I suppose that was the first time that I had
heard of Guiana, but father told me more about
it when the candles were lit in the evening. I
don't know how much I understood. It was so
like a fairy-tale, a story of the quest for el
Dorado, of a great river where quartz glittered
in the sand like diamonds, of Indians with gold
in their ears and round their necks, of a strange
horned beast, called the armadillo, and of
women who fought like men. The details have
slipped from my mind, but I do remember my
father tapping the table and saying, 'And when
they came within sight of the mountains, Sir
Walter found a bag of refiner's tools in a bush.

Then, he knew that he was right. Somewhere, if only he could find it, there was a rich gold-mine.' I've forgotten the rest. I only know that they had to come home before they had found the mine, and that was the end of the story. I cried then, partly because I was sorry for their disappointment and partly because I had been born a maid instead of a lad and could never have such adventures.

"I dreamed of gold-mines that night, and I think Sir Walter must have dreamed of them, too, every night of his thirteen years' captivity, for they say that he was always urging the King to let him go back to Guiana.

"Then, two years ago, came the news. I remember it well because I was ten that day. Father came in and kissed me suddenly on both cheeks, and I was startled because that was not his way. He usually waited for me to kneel for his blessing and sometimes kissed me after-wards. But he rumpled my hair and laughed: 'I've birthday tidings for you, Meg. Sir Walter's out.' I was so excited that I danced round and round the table, till mother said I made her giddy and sent me to fetch the servants and offer them each a mug of sack. Although it was my birthday, we drank Sir Walter's health first, and then mine. Then we went down to the river to find the old waterman and father gave him some money to celebrate the occasion.

He grinned, showing his toothless gums, and all the skin round his eyes wrinkled up like a withered leaf. I was frightened, a little, when he bent forward, because he was so dirty and I thought he was going to kiss my hand. But he didn't. He just spat twice on the coin and rubbed it on the back of his breeches, mumbling something about 'Good luck in Guiana.'

"After that the whole talk was of Guiana for months and months and I think I prayed every night that Sir Walter should find his mine. Of course, there were conditions attached to his going, for the King hadn't pardoned him, really. He had graciously permitted his captive freedom provided he brought back the treasure and didn't interfere with the Spaniards. How father's lip curled when he told me! He said that Queen Bess would turn in her grave if she knew how the King fawned on the Spanish ambassador.

"Of course, you know what happened. He came back a broken man, his son killed, and his seamen mutinous. He hadn't found the mine.

"They say that ill-news travels apace, and the tidings reached London before Sir Walter landed at Plymouth. What an ado! It set the whole town talking. The very pedlars in the streets pretended to have news and sold false secrets to earn dishonest pence. As for the court, men say it was in a ferment—horror,

THE SECOND PART OF VOX POPVLI,
OR
Gondomar appearing in the likenes of
Matchiauell in a Spanish Parliament,
wherein are discouered his treacherous & subtile Practises
To the ruine as well of England as the Netherlandes.
Faithfully Translated out of the Spanish Coppie by a well-willer
to England and Holland.

The second
Edition.

BIBL
CANT.
ACAD.

Simul Complectar omnia

Gentis Hispanæ decus

"That beast Gondomar"

satisfaction, scorn, fear—everything —his friends grieved and anxious, and that beast Gondomar, the Spaniard, rushing into the King's chamber, shouting, ' Pirates! Pirates! Pirates!' Then the clanging of the bells and everyone running into the public squares and gaping at the street corners, while the heralds and the criers shouted the proclamation about 'a horrible invasion of the town of San Thomé.' They must have hated their work that day, for the common people hissed and booed them when they pronounced Sir Walter and his companions traitors 'for a malicious breaking of the peace which hath been so happily established and so long inviolately continued.'

"Pirates and traitors, forsooth, because they burned and looted a Spanish city! Could they do otherwise when it stood between them and the mine? Could they leave unavenged an attack on their own camp? Father says they were right. He says that the land round the Orinoco is ours, that in 1595 Queen Bess gave Sir Walter a commission to annex and colonise it. That was the first time that he went to Guiana, and the Spanish city has been built since then.

"I don't understand it all, for some say one thing and some another and I can't piece the story together. But why blame Sir Walter for an expedition that failed? Was it his fault that

he lay sick and had to let another lead his men?
Could he stop them from burning the city when
he wasn't there? Could he help it if they came
back without finding the mine?

"I think it broke father's heart, for he's
never been the same since the trial. He went
down to Westminster Hall and heard the sentence and saw the guards, sixty of them, taking
Sir Walter to the Gatehouse, and Lady Ralegh
in her coach, looking like death. Then he came
home. I was frightened when I saw him, for he
looked quite old and haggard and the light
seemed to have gone out of his eyes. Mother
raised her brows in a silent question, but he
didn't say very much. He just nodded and
whispered, 'To-morrow, in the old Palace
Yard.'

"For a few minutes nobody spoke; then
mother told me to go to bed, and for some
reason I was afraid of my own shadow, which
looked so black on the panelling as I went upstairs with my candle.

"I pulled my little truckle bed from under
the big one and undressed, but I couldn't rest,
and long after father and mother had come up
and had fallen asleep, I lay awake staring in the
darkness at the ceiling. We had clean sheets
that night, and they smelt of a powder of flags
which Bet often sprinkles in the press. It was
a cool smell, really, but I felt hot and miserable

and twice I got up and pushed open the casement to look out. It was very still. The penthouses opposite looked like the peaked ears of some huge animal, and the moon made a pool of light on the cobbles, where I saw our watchman asleep, huddled in his cloak with his club at his side. Then the bellman passed with his dog and I heard his voice, coming nearer and nearer, then fading away:

> Give ear to the clock!
> Beware your lock,
> Your fire and your light,
> And God give you good-night!

"I pulled in the casement and went back to bed. '*God give you good-night.*' What would his last night be like?

"I think it was then that I made up my mind: I knew it would be disobedient, for I am never allowed to go out alone, partly because it is unseemly and partly because of the rogues and vagabonds who roam through the smaller streets and outside the city. But I am nearly twelve, old enough to take care of myself and too old to be punished, though mother still keeps a rod in her closet to whip our maidens when they are idle.

"I thought I would risk a scolding. It was worth it. After all, he was father's hero and I had never even seen him, though all these years I had toyed with the thought of him and my mind had painted his picture. It was my only chance.

"After that I felt quite quiet and I fell asleep till a thin streak of light coming through a crack in the shutter shone across my pillow and woke me next morning. Father and mother were dreaming with the curtains drawn closely round their bed, and there was scarcely a sound outside. It didn't take me a minute to dress, and I pulled out the pin and crept from the room with the stairs going 'creak-creak-creak' under my bare feet and my shoes and pattens in my hand.

"I struggled with the door and it rattled, making my heart beat so fast for fear I should be heard, that I felt almost faint. The bar was heavy and I had to balance it on my shoulder while I was pulling it back, and the key was so stiff that it blistered both my hands, but I managed to turn it and slip out. I put on my shoes and pattens in the street and ran, holding my hood over my face. Some apprentices called after me and one seized my cloak, but I twitched it out of his hand and never stopped running till I came to the river.

"Our waterman was there crying 'Westward ho!' to the market-women who had come in betimes with their fowls. He shook his head when I told him what I wanted, muttering, 'Little maids should be abed,' and he was all for taking me back to father, but I gave him my amber

necklace and cut short his mumbling by jumping into the boat and unhitching the rope from
the post. He got wet scrambling after me, but
he pushed off with his oar and rowed towards
Westminster. I think he told me how wilful
lassies were treated in his young days, but I
wasn't listening. I was watching the reflection
of the Tower in the river and how it trembled
when our oars rippled the surface of the water.

"I shall never forget that day. It was the
twenty-ninth of October, one of those autumn
mornings when everything looks cool and wet
and the sunshine is silver instead of gold. It all
seemed strangely quiet. I could only hear the
splash of the oars. None of the birds were
singing and there wasn't a breath of wind to
stir the trees. The leaves had begun to turn.
The beeches were brown and the chestnuts and
planes all yellow with a little rim of light round
their edges, and I kept wondering what it
would be like to see them for the last time.

"The waterman must have been rowing
slowly, for it seemed so long before we reached
the wharf at Westminster. I think I was dazed
or weary from rising so early, because I
stumbled as he steadied the boat for me, and he
frowned a little anxiously and tapped my
shoulder, saying 'Don't ye tarry when it's
over. I'll row ye home.' When I looked back
he was still watching me.

"I suppose they had arranged that the execution should be in the morning, because it was Lord Mayor's Day and they were afraid of the crowds; but early as it was, there was a throng of people pushing and jostling in front of the Parliament House, and when I tried to squeeze through to the old Palace Yard, the smell of frieze and fustian made me feel sick. I wished I had been wearing chopines to make me taller, and then I could have seen over the heads of the people without trying to get in front. As it was, I had to thrust with my hands and elbows because I was in danger of being crushed. One man picked me up by the waist and pushed me quite near to the scaffold, but when I turned to thank him, he shook me as though I were a naughty child, saying 'Go to! Thou little hussy. This is no place for a maid,' till I edged away in a fright.

"But I wasn't the only maid. There were others in the crowd and ladies of fashion, too. I knew them for their cloaks belled out over their farthingales, and I saw the paint on their lips and cheeks though they'd hidden their eyes under black vizard masks. There were lords on horseback not far from the scaffold, and Sir Randolph Carew's balcony was packed. I remember thinking that the gentlemen looked like wizards in their long velvet robes and high-crowned hats.

"When I arrived, men were still hammering at the scaffold, for they had built it overnight in a hurry, but the headsman and his attendant were already there by the block. They were masked and in black, like the demons which one sees in a nightmare, and they'd covered the axe with a cloak.

"It was all nearly as quiet as the river. One could only hear the taps of the hammer, the heavy breathing of that jostling crowd and the crackle of the faggots, where the sheriffs had lighted a fire by the scaffold and were huddling over it warming their hands.

"We waited while time seemed to crawl. Then they fetched him. I was nearly knocked down, for the crowd surged forward bursting the barriers, and his guards had to join hands to prevent him from being swept off his feet.

"I was watching, breathless with the struggle and excitement, when suddenly I saw that he was old. I suppose I ought to have known it, but, somehow, I had always imagined him young and strong with a dark pointed beard and the gay bright clothes of a courtier. This was an old man, with curly white hair and a pale face, wrinkled and furrowed. He walked with a stoop and his knees trembled, for he had ague, but his eyes were steady, and when the people cried 'Good cheer, Sir Walter!' he raised a hand in greeting and turned to the

Dean of Westminster who walked behind and whispered something, smiling.

"He was breathless when he reached the scaffold, for the pressure of the crowd was terrible, and he sat for a minute while the sheriffs began to murmur and talk. I think they must have fetched him from his bed, for a black velvet night-robe covered his hair-coloured satin doublet and black waistcoat, and his hat was over a wrought lace night-cap. I don't think I should have noticed the night-cap if he had not taken off his hat and called to the old, bald-headed man standing next to me, 'Why have you come here, in this inclement weather? Would you have anything of me?' And the old man answered in a quavering voice, 'Nothing, Sir Walter, nothing! I have but come to see you and to pray for you.' Sir Walter thanked him, saying 'I grieve that I have no better return to make you for your goodwill than this, which you need, my friend, more than I.' He threw his night-cap to the old man and somebody behind caught it and pulled it over the bald head.

"I wished that I could have had it. I wanted something which had belonged to him, but I hadn't much time for wishing, for the sheriffs were making their proclamation and immediately afterwards Sir Walter stood up and began to speak. I don't know how long he was talking—

I think about three-quarters of an hour, but the crowd was so still that you could have heard a pin fall, and everyone gazed at him, hanging on his lips.

"I cannot repeat what he said for I have but a poor memory for words. I only know that he began in a very low voice, saying, 'I thank God that he has sent me to die in the light and not in the darkness, before such an assembly of honourable witnesses....' Then he began to disprove all the vile charges which had been brought against him, denying that he had plotted with France, denying that he had invented the gold-mine in Guiana that he might recover his liberty. I saw his eyes sadden when he begged all to believe that he had never sought the death of Essex, nor puffed tobacco from a window as he watched his execution. The crowd murmured at that. There was not a man in that great throng who could think him capable of such baseness. When he spoke of the King, I felt the tears welling up into my eyes. So gentle to a King who had trodden on his dreams! I can hear him now, a little husky but every word distinct and true. 'It is no time for me to flatter or to fear princes, I who am subject only unto death; yet if ever I spoke dishonestly of the King, the Lord blot me out of the book of life.'

"He paused for a minute and, after begging us to join with him in prayer, he waved and smiled, saying 'I have a long journey to take and must bid the company farewell.'

"At that my knees began to shake and some-body put out an arm to support me. The people were silent. They looked dead, and their eyes never moved while Sir Walter was unfastening his ruff and laying aside his robe and doublet. When he stood there, hatless, a tall bent figure in ash-coloured stockings, taffeta breeches and silk shirt, he called for the axe. I felt frightened, as though something inside me were being pulled so tightly that it would burst, and I shivered when he felt the edge. But he only nodded his head and the white curls shook. 'Ah,' he said, 'this gives me no fear. 'Tis a sharp and fair medicine to cure me of all my diseases.' Then he turned to the headsman, 'When I stretch forth my hands, dispatch me,' he said. I think the headsman was unmanned, for I saw a tear slide from under his mask and he took off his own cloak and spread it for Sir Walter to kneel upon. But he knelt himself, first, asking forgiveness, only my heart was beating so loudly that I could not hear what he said. I saw Sir Walter put his hand on his shoulder and pat it gently, then kneel before the block, but I suppose that something was wrong, for he rose again and laughed, then knelt facing the east, saying, 'What matter how the head lie so the heart be right?'

"The executioner wanted to blindfold him,

but he shook his head, laughing. 'Think you I fear the shadow of the axe when I fear not itself?' Then he looked down and for one minute his eyes, like mirrors of light, gazed straight into mine, and he said 'Give me heartily of your prayers.'

"I don't really know what happened, for I covered my face with my hands and every prayer that I could remember raced through my mind, a strange medley of words that had no meaning yet meant so much. I said nothing aloud, but caught myself whispering 'Amen, Amen, Amen' over and over again. As I did so a clear voice spoke from the scaffold, saying 'What dost thou fear? Strike man, strike.'

"I heard two thuds and opened my eyes.

"The trunk lay on the scaffold in a pool of blood. Above the faces of the people stretched the black arm of the executioner, and a voice which seemed to be making some great effort said 'This is the head of a traitor.'

"Nobody answered, but through the crowd a terrible shudder passed like a wave and from the balcony a woman moaned.

"People say that the head was put in a red leather bag and sent in a mourning coach to Lady Ralegh, while the Dean and his friends carried the body to St Margaret's Church. This may be true, but I didn't see and I cannot remember what I did. I think that I waited long after the crowd had gone and that the old waterman came to find me. I know that he put me at the bottom of the boat, and I lay there listening to the splash of the water and the distant sound of trumpets, for the ridings had begun.

"My mother said nothing when I came in. She knew where I had been. And I stood in the doorway with my cloak trailing in the rushes and my eyes fixed on my father. He was sitting on a joint-stool with his arms stretched across the table and his head buried in them. He looked up when I touched him. 'It's finished,' I said, and he strode past me through the door muttering, 'A craven sacrifice to Spain.'

"I think something happened to me then, for though I was crying I felt that I was going to laugh and I kept saying, 'Amen, Amen, Amen' till mother hurried me up to bed and gave me a hot posset.

"I lay there shivering and crying for days, and I thought that my father was angry for he never came near me.

"Then one afternoon when I had dressed for the first time, and was sitting at the window, he came and took my hand.

"'They are selling ballads in the street,' he said, 'and I've brought back a verse for you.' He pulled a cushion into the window seat and read with his arm round my shoulder:

Great Heart, who taught thee so to die?
Death yielding thee the victory.
When tookst thou leave of life? If there,
How cams't thou then so free from fear?
Sure thou didst die and quit the fate
Of flesh and blood before that state.
I saw in all the standers by
Pale Death, life only in thine eye.
Farewell, Truth shall this story say—
We died, thou only livedst that day.

"We were silent for a few minutes, then Father folded the verse and put it into his bible: 'They should write that on Sir Walter's tomb,' he said.

"But I am not sure. I think, somehow, that his own words make the better epitaph: 'What matter how the head lie so the heart be right?'"

CHAPTER X

FROM CHRIST'S HOSPITAL TO SURAT

[A.D. 1668. Cession of Bombay to the East India Company]

Hubert squirmed. There were pins and needles in his toes and whenever he moved, James, who was lying beside him, grunted crossly and turned over, taking far more than his share of the bed, so that Hubert was obliged to cling to the edge, where each blade of straw seemed to be poking through the mattress into his skin. He wriggled and attempted to kick his bed-fellow, but when one has cramp a successful kick is almost impossible, so he tried the old charm which every Blue-Coat boy had used since Edward VI had founded Christ's Hospital more than a century earlier. With his thumb against his back teeth he whispered over and over again:

> Foot, foot, foot is fast asleep,
> Thumb, thumb, thumb in spittle we steep!
> Crosses three we make to ease us,
> Two for the thieves and one for Christ Jesus!

But it was useless. The pins and needles pricked more unpleasantly than ever, and Hubert rolled out of bed and hopped round the dormitory holding his foot and grumbling, "Ah—oooh! Ah—oooh!"

One by one his companions awoke. Fair and

dark heads bobbed up from straw-filled pillows, arms stretched, mouths gaped widely in yawns, and anxious voices asked "Is it six o'clock?" "Has the usher rung the bell?"

"No, no," gasped Hubert, still gripping his toes and chanting, "*Foot, foot, foot is fast asleep.*"

His face was agonised, but his companions had no mercy, and pillows followed the imprecations which were hurled at his head.

On Monday mornings, nobody liked being awakened earlier than was necessary. It was a barren day full of uninteresting lessons and empty of good meals. On most days the monotonous breakfast of two and a half ounces of bread and "a sup of drink" was followed by meat either at noon or at night, but on Monday supper consisted of cheese, and there was nothing for dinner but water-gruel and currants. And so it was pleasant to lie abed, half-asleep, pretending unreasonably that it was still Sunday, when there would be no lessons but a hearty meal of boiled beef, porridge and five ounces of bread at noon, and the public supping of roast mutton at night.

To be wakened simply because Hubert had cramp was annoying, but the boys might have spared themselves the trouble of silencing him, for no sooner had they thrown the last pillow than the rising bell rang and everyone leaped out of bed.

The dressing which followed was rather more hurried than usual. The boys were supposed to make their beds before going to the Writing School for prayers, and of course this could not be done until all the pillows, which had been scattered about the room, were collected. While James, Hubert and the others were buttoning themselves into their long blue coats or pulling over their heads those shapeless yellow petticoats known as kersies, the smallest boy in the room was threatened with dire penalties if he did not gather together the pillows and smooth as many coverlets as possible, before his elders were ready. He began to sniff and whine, for he was a good little boy who never willingly broke a rule, but the escapades of his comrades had so often made him late for roll-call that scarcely a week passed without his feeling the full rigour of the law "if any shall be missing, correction shall be given him by shame or smart." Luckily Hubert had a kind heart and quick fingers with button-holes and strings, so that he was soon ready to lend a hand, and roll-call was brought to a satisfactory close.

After this, Bible-reading, lessons and the nauseous swallowing of water-gruel and currants passed without mishap, and Hubert began to feel quite cheerful. Usually James and he

looked upon the cramps as a bad omen and believed, like every old gossip in the country,

> By the pricking of my thumbs
> Something evil this way comes.

All, however, seemed to be going well and it
was only in the afternoon that their hearts sank.
They were having a writing lesson, and that day
they were copying the "Rule for scholars":

> Ink alwais good store on right hand to stand,
> Brown paper for haste or else box of sand;
> Dip pen and shake pen and touch pen for haire,
> Wax, quills and pen-knife see alwais ye beare.

The curves of the small letters were even, the
up-strokes and down-strokes were thick or fine
according to the master's rule, and each capital
had that graceful flourish which every other
boy envied. They knew that their master would
be pleased and so they nearly fell off their stools
with astonishment when the usher came in,
called out their names with six others, telling
each horrified boy to await the master in his
private chamber.

Hubert looked at his companions as they dis-
mally filed out of the Writing School and avoided
the sympathetic glances of the other boys who
remained on their benches, heartily thankful
that they had been spared such an interview.

"Why?" whispered Hubert, thinking without any difficulty of several undiscovered crimes.

"What for?" muttered James, who was next to him. Among them all they could furnish so many excellent reasons that their courage ebbed away, and they slunk down the narrow staircase, eight forlorn little scholars, whose imaginations, stimulated by experience, were unpleasantly vivid.

Nervously clutching their long coats and hitching up their yellow petticoats, which were so generously cut that they allowed for growing and not for hurrying, the boys arrived at the heavy oak door. On most occasions it looked formidable, but to-day the black marks, showing where the flames had scorched it two years before in the Great Fire, seemed darker than ever and gave it a frowning appearance. It was obviously somebody's duty to tap and lift the latch when the master said "come in." But there was such a shuffling of feet, such a pushing and a scuffling and such an agitated whispering of "You-go-first"—"No-you," that the door

A Christ's Hospital boy

was opened, suddenly and impatiently, from within. Framed in the archway stood the familiar figure of the master, and farther back in the room a stranger was seated, cross-kneed, on a cushioned joint-stool. He was a man of fashion or wealth, from the top of his long curling wig to the soles of his grey silk stockings. His satin waistcoat was garnished with silver buttons, and the frills which hung from his cuffs and knee-breeches were of the finest white lace. His purple felt hat lay on his knees and he was curling the feather round his fingers while his lips twitched with amusement.

"A visit to the master's chamber seems a matter for dread," said he, as the boys sidled into the room, blushing with confusion. "And what," he asked, pretending to look severe and shaking his new-fashioned rattan at Hubert, "have you done to be spared Jeremiah's vision of the whacking-rod?"

Hubert grinned sheepishly, but his spirits rose and he nudged James. His quick eyes had espied a sample of his own writing on the table. He remembered having gained full marks for that piece, so obviously it could not entitle him either to a "shame or smart" and he felt relieved. The stranger followed the direction of his glance and laughed again. "So," he said, "you think that the up-strokes and down-strokes of your pens should stand between you and similar strokes of yonder weapon in the corner?" The boys tried to look unconcerned, but their eyes roved irresistibly towards the birch-rod which always seemed the most conspicuous object in the room, and the stranger watched them, twinkling. "Well, well!" he said, "I am of a like mind about that penmanship." He patted Hubert on the shoulder and turned to the master. "'Tis agreed, then? These eight boys. The two best at the next sailing!"

He nodded pleasantly and swaggered towards the door, so that the black curls of his wig danced and the full skirts of his purple laced coat swayed rhythmically from hip to knee. As he passed the birch-rod he paused for a minute shaking his head, then he flicked it with his rattan and murmuring "Oh, Solomon, Solomon!" left the room, while the boys stood quite still staring at him and forgetting, in their astonishment, that good manners should have prompted them to open the door.

The master was apparently pleased, for he rubbed his hands and looked with an air of satisfaction at his pupils and the specimens of hand-writing before him. Then, with a few preliminary remarks as to "good conduct," "a fair round-hand," "the honour of the school" and "the reputation of Christ's Hospital at the other ends of the earth," he announced the purpose of the stranger's visit. The *Honourable Company of Merchants of England Trading to the East Indies* had engaged eight Blue-Coat boys to serve as apprentices in their factory at Surat, and later to become "writers" or "penmen" at a salary of £10 a year.

The boys looked at one another, glowing with pride. They knew all about the East India Company and they imagined that the gentleman was one of the governors who had come straight from the East India House with the message. That house, with all its little wooden pillars and leaded panes, with the busy coming and going through its doors, had always interested them, and whenever they had marched through Leadenhall Street, under the stern eye of their usher, they had been tempted to stop and stare at it. The ships painted below the coping and the carved dolphins on the roof fascinated them, while to the wooden figure of the merchant which surmounted the whole building and was outlined so arrogantly against the sky, they had given the nickname "The King of Leadenhall Street." To have been asked to work in the East India House would have been a compliment, but to be sent to India for the company was not only a compliment but an adventure.

The boys thought of the voyage and the cargo which their ship would carry, nothing very romantic, but useful goods such as broad-

The old East India House

cloth, silk and woollen stockings, garters, ribands, beaver and felt hats, strong waters, knives, Spanish leather shoes and looking-glasses. Then they remembered all the delightful things which came to England from the East, and wondered whether they would help to store them in the factory of the East India Company at Surat, or pack them into the ships' holds. There would be cloves and cinnamon, long pepper and white pepper, white powdered sugar, preserved nutmegs and ginger, drugs of all sorts, musk, aloes, ambergris, bezoar-stones and agateheads. Perhaps some of the ships would go farther afield and bring back rich carpets of Persia and Cambay, satin and taffeta quilts, painted calicoes and damask, porcelain dishes and all the luxuries to which Englishmen had grown so used. Each boy drew a deep breath, but six faces fell when the master announced that James and Hubert, being the best writers, had been chosen to go first.

James's eyes sparkled with pleasure, but Hubert felt proud. He was the better penman of the two and to him was given the honour of thanking the great Company for their courtesy. With a solemn face he remained in the master's room, carefully pointing a new quill pen. Then, with the tip of his tongue between his lips and his hand moving slowly and deliberately, he conveyed to the Company the thanks of the governors for having been "pleased to take off from the charge of this hospitall eight children to be employed in their affaires beyound the seas and had att great charges clothed and provided necessaries for these children's voyage."

How the boys enjoyed that voyage! For the first time, they were wearing coats, knee-breeches and waistcoats; simple garments it is true, but very different from the long blue cassocks lined with Welsh cotton, the yellow petticoats, white neck-bands and small round caps to which they were accustomed. For the first time, they made friends with sailors and cabin boys and learned strange tales of sea-serpents. For the first time, they copied lists of cargo and wrote at the dictation of someone who was not a school-master. They were servants of the great East India Company.

The captain of the ship was a servant of the Company, too, and as such he made a point of telling the new apprentices all about Surat, with its factory of stone and timber built in the Moorish style, its galleries, oratory and large public dining-hall. The boys listened with rapt attention as he described the spacious lodgings of the president, with the pleasant tanks of cool water, the courtyards and separate bath-house. And they grew almost impatient, longing to arrive, when he talked to them of the dark-skinned traders, who presented themselves from ten till noon and sometimes from four till midnight, all round the lower floor of the factory, where the goods were stored.

James and Hubert sighed, longing to be the factors who would interview these Indian traders, instead of apprentices in a humble position. But the captain comforted them. "Creep before you walk! Walk before you run! From apprentice to writer (that's an important post because then you'll copy letters and consultations)! From writer to factor, from factor to merchant! What more do you want?"

The boys agreed that the result of being an apprentice was satisfactory, but when they heard about all the rules which they had to obey, they began to feel nervous. If one stayed out after the gate was shut, between eight and nine, one was fined. Absence from prayers meant a fine of 2s. 6d. on week-days and 5s. on Sundays. Striking or abusing persons not in the company's service meant three days' imprisonment in irons. There was a Black Book for offences and a White Book for faithful services. At this the two boys looked dismal. If the president exercised such authority over the apprentices and men under his roof, they began to think that they might just as well have remained at Christ's Hospital under a school-master.

Seeing their gloomy faces, the captain began to extol the Company, telling them how proud he was of being its servant, how its position in India was improving slowly but surely, and how little by little, in spite of the Dutch and the Portuguese, its foothold was becoming firmer. He rubbed his hands and wagged a wise head at James. "What do you think we're carrying in the *Constantinople Merchant*?" said he.

Both boys promptly answered "Cargo," and the captain laughed.

"Cargo," he said, "but something else, too! We carry a document." He rubbed his hands again and winked knowingly at Hubert, who looked mystified.

"Aah!" said the captain, poking a long finger into the boy's ribs. "What d'you think of that? A document! A Royal Charter transferring the island of Bombay from the Crown to the Company."

Both boys looked blank and the captain threw up his hands in horror. "What," he cried, "you don't mean to tell me that you are servants of the Company and you know nothing about Bombay? You don't know about the marriage treaty between His Majesty King Charles II and the Infanta of Portugal! Well, well, well!" He shook his head and looked at the young apprentices severely. "Why, what did they teach you at school? Haven't you learned that the port and island of Bombay, with all the rights, profits and territories belonging to it, were handed over to King Charles and his heirs, in 1661! In my opinion" (here he winked again) "'twas the best part of Señora Catherine's dowry. And, bless you, the Portuguese knew it, too. *They* weren't over-pleased when their King gave it to Britain." He paused for a minute and tried to look grave. "Far be it from me to be disloyal," said he, "but King Charles doesn't really know its value. He thinks it will be an expense, so what does he do but offer it to the East India Company, at a rent of £10 a year in gold. And what does the Company do but" (here he took off his hat with a flourish and made a low bow) "accept with pleasure."

At this interesting piece of information James and Hubert forgot their anxiety about the rules and the Black Book, and whenever the captain was at leisure they asked him to tell them about Bombay.

To boys who had never been beyond London, the stories of the six islands around Bombay, the swamps of samphire and the groves of coco-nut trees, were like scenes in some romance. They never tired of listening to tales about the fishermen's huts thatched with palm-leaves, the little Portuguese houses tiled and glazed with oyster-shells and the churches of Jesuit and Franciscan. But best of all they loved to hear about the people. There were Portuguese landowners who would now pay a rent to the English, and half-castes who were partly Indian and partly Portuguese yet looked like neither. There were Kolis, who cultivated the fields or lived in a small group of rude dwellings near the custom-house and spent their time fishing. There were a few Parsees, who worshipped fire, and Bhandaris, who earned a living by tapping the palm-trees and distilling liquor.

It was delightful to know that this romantic island, with its useful port, its strange people and all its possibilities of trade, was to become the property of the East India Company. As servants of that company, James and Hubert felt that they had some small share in the transaction, and it was a proud moment when they stepped ashore at Surat, knowing that they had arrived in the same ship as the Royal Charter.

Indeed, they were so much interested in all the gossip and excitement about Bombay, that for the first three weeks they scarcely noticed how steadily their noses were kept to the grindstone, nor how many and strict were the rules which they were expected to obey.

When the great day came for the *Constantinople Merchant* to sail to Bombay, the two young apprentices took a personal pride in her mission. Down to the shore they ran and mingled with the crowd of onlookers. The moment was too solemn for them to wave, as they were tempted, to their old friend the captain, for no sooner had they arrived at the water's edge than a sound of trumpets filled the air, and through the gates of the factory came Sir George Oxenden, President of Surat.

With his eyes proudly gazing at the ship, he was borne in a gilded palanquin preceded by a horse of state in the gayest of trappings. An Indian boy, dressed in scarlet and white, kept the sun from his face by an immense fan of ostrich feathers. On each side strode a guard of English soldiers in double file. Two flags were carried before him, and behind came the chaplain and the physician, followed by the factors on horseback and the three gentlemen who were to represent the president and receive Bombay on behalf of the Company.

The boys watched the procession with eager eyes and listened with pride to the president's speech as he bade farewell to his three agents.

They did not speak, but they clasped each other's hands when with a flourish of trumpets the flag was hoisted to the *Constantinople Merchant's* mast, the guns from the fort fired a salute, and dipping through the water the ship slowly sailed for Bombay.

In the gathering darkness the president was borne in his palanquin to the factory. Merchants, factors and writers strolled back to their tasks, murmuring "new trade," "a firmer foothold," and the native population, a dusky medley of Arab, Hindu, Koli and Bhandari, left, chattering and gesticulating, for their homes.

Only Hubert and James remained on the shore. Shading their eyes with their hands, they watched the black silhouette of the *Constantinople Merchant* until she became a speck on the horizon.

"Bombay!" whispered James and stopped in horror, for Hubert who had been standing for too long in one position wore a twisted expression of agony.

"Ah—ooh! Ah—ooh!" he cried, grasping his foot and hopping,

The devil is tying a knot in my leg!
Mark, Luke and John unloose it I beg.

And James, thinking of evil omens, heard the factory gate clang, and murmured mournfully,

Crosses three we make to ease us,
Two for the thieves and one for Christ Jesus.

CHAPTER XI

THE STRANGE WHITE BIRD

[A.D. 1769. James Cook comes to New Zealand]

It was a beautiful evening. The sea sparkled like a cut sapphire, and a cool wind stirred its surface so that the flecks of foam seemed to be dancing away to the horizon. Behind the cliffs lay the forest, a deep noiseless jungle where the bright green of fern and shrub hid the trunks of pine and beech tree, and here and there a glimmer of flowers flashed, crimson and white, in the undergrowth. The distant mountains, with their peaks delicately pencilled against the sky, looked like clouds, and the air was very soft and fragrant.

But Horeta Taniwha, fourth son of a Maori tribesman, neither saw nor felt the beauty of his native land. His lower lip hung down. His cheeks were dirty with rings of half-dried tears and his fat little ivory-coloured body drooped with dejection.

His name, Horeta Taniwha, meant "the red-smeared dragon," but at that moment there was nothing very fierce or dragon-like in his appearance, and the only smears came from his own grimy hands. He was eight years old, almost old enough to cease being naked like the younger children, and to wear a waist-mat of

undressed flax like his brothers. But Taniwha
had forgotten his eight years. He sat on the floor
with his back to the open doorway and his face
to the reed-covered walls, looking rather like a
sulky baby. Early that morning his father and
his brothers had taken the new canoe and gone
fishing. They had not even suggested that
Taniwha should see it launched, but had
thrown him the skeletons of some birds and a
pile of barbed wood and told him to make fish-
hooks.

Taniwha stared resentfully at the pointed
mussel shells and the sharp flint-stones which
were his tools. He had not begun to work.
Crying had made him hiccough and one needed
a steady hand for fish-hooks. Besides, it was
unfair to set him a task when the others were
enjoying themselves. It was not as though he
had not helped to make the canoe. He had even
thought of its name, Ao-réré, "the flying cloud,"
and although he had not been able to do any of
the carving, he had spent many a long hour
collecting the gay feathers and the mother-o'-
pearl, and drying the strips of flax with which
the side of the canoe had been decorated.

The little boy choked when he thought of it
and scattered the heap of wood with an angry
thrust of his foot.

"Taniwha!" cried a warning voice.

Taniwha did not answer. He eyed the

scattered chips askance and, still squatting by the wall, wriggled round until he faced the door.

"Taniwha!" cried the voice again, and this time it was followed by the impatient padding of bare feet across the wooden verandah. Taniwha began to breathe quickly. His mother was coming. He knew her voice and her heavy step. He could see her bare legs and the flapping ends of her waist-mat before he saw her face, because the floor on which he sat had been dug below the level of the ground. Taniwha watched her stoop and step down into the hut. Her thick, dark hair fell forward and she put one hand behind her to steady the baby, which was slung in a mat on her back and partly covered by her own feathery cloak.

She glanced first at the untidy floor and then at Taniwha, who was poking his big toe in and out of a hole in the flax matting.

"Your fish-hooks?" she asked.

Taniwha thrust out his lower lip and scowled as his mother began to gather up the pieces of barbed wood. "When Rona was angry and made faces," said the woman, "the moon punished her."

"Tell!" ordered Taniwha, grumpy but interested.

"Rona was a beautiful girl. One night she had to go into the forest to fetch water. She took up her calabash and stole out. At first she had no trouble in finding the way, because the moon was shining. But when she came to the thickest part, where the stones were sharpest and the ferns and shrubs all tangled together, the moon disappeared behind a cloud. Rona stumbled and cut her foot on a rock. 'Come out, you!' she cried to the moon. But the moon still hid her face and Rona stumbled again. Then she lost her temper. 'You stupid old tattoo-face, come out!' she shouted, stamping her foot and making a hideous grimace. Just as she did so the cloud drifted away from the moon and Rona felt herself floating up in the air. Up, up, up, she went until she reached the tops of the trees. She screamed and seized some branches to save herself, but up came the tree by the roots and floated higher and higher. Rona never went home again. She was punished for getting angry and making faces. To-night if you look up at the sky you'll see her, calabash, thorn tree and all, hanging in front of the moon!"

Taniwha drew a deep breath. He had often looked at the moon and seen something like the figure of a woman with a calabash and a tree, so the story must be true. He snatched up a mussel shell and began to scrape a piece of wood into a fish-hook. "Didn't make faces at the moon. Didn't call her names," he said sulkily.

"It is well," answered his mother, and she

picked up a gourd full of fern roots and took them on to the wooden platform in front of the door and began to pound them into powder. They were for Taniwha's supper. She herself would have some dog's flesh, which was steaming over the red-hot stones in the little oven outside the house.

But Taniwha was not thinking of supper. His mind was busy with the story of Rona. Was it fun up there by the stars? Did Rona like living among the clouds? Taniwha frowned. He supposed there were houses and canoes up there. After all, his own country was called Ao-tea-roa, "the long white cloud," and life in one cloud was probably much the same as in another. But the moon? Ah, that might be different. He wondered whether Rona were happy. And her brothers, had they been sorry when they saw her hanging there every night, and making no attempt to come home? Taniwha sat up suddenly and smiled. He had an idea. What if *he* were to make faces and scold the moon? He could always play with Rona once he was there, and perhaps if his father and his brothers saw him hanging in the sky, so far away, they would be sorry that they had not taken him fishing.

The idea pleased Taniwha. He grinned happily, put the finished fish-hook into a hollow gourd and strolled out to his supper.

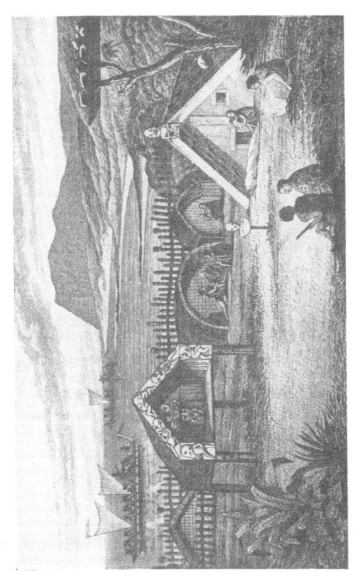

A Maori *pa*

The *pa*, as the Maori village was called, was humming with talk and laughter, for most of the children and the old women were seated outside their houses eating and chattering while flies buzzed about their heads. Here and there a young woman was busy with some household task. One was dyeing reeds to renew the lining of her walls; another was scraping the fibre of the palm-lily with a pointed stone, so that when it was ready she could make it into a mat. Taniwha watched from a distance. He wondered whether Rona had to work up there in the moon. Did she gather flax and make it into mantles? Taniwha hoped not, for then he might have to help her, and working with flax never seemed to end. First the blades had to be gathered and soaked till the green covering was soft. Then they were beaten with a stone pounder and washed outside the *pa* in a stream till all the waste matter had floated away and the fibre was exposed. Taniwha frowned when he thought of that fibre. If he were not making fish-hooks, or collecting mother-o'-pearl shells for someone's canoe, he was always being called to help with the flax fibre, which had to be scraped before it could be woven into waist-mats. If Rona wanted him to do that, he would refuse. After all, she was only a naughty girl who was still being punished, so he need not obey her.

He sighed with relief. It was comforting to think that he need stand no nonsense from Rona. His difficulty at the moment was to escape into the woods without being seen. He could not possibly make faces at the moon from his own house. He looked round cautiously.

A Maori woman weaving a flax mat

Every one was busy. Should he dart suddenly or stroll casually in the direction of the gate? He decided on the latter course and, still scraping at a fish-hook, he walked carelessly towards the double palisade which surrounded the *pa*.

It was unfortunate that Te Pou the *tattoo* artist was sitting outside his house. Taniwha rubbed his eyes furtively and hoped that the tears had not left any stains. Te Pou had a great scorn for boys who cried. He was used to seeing people bear pain without flinching, for he tattooed the face of every man in the tribe, cutting and pricking the tender flesh inch by inch with the tiny wing bones of a sea-bird, then wiping away the blood and injecting the blue dye which smarted so painfully. Sometimes it took him several weeks or even months to finish a face, and all the time that he was making the design of curves and spirals, the patient showed no sign of pain. If he had flinched, he would have been a disgrace to the tribe. Boys who cried easily might groan or wince when they were being tattooed, so the old man was forever testing their endurance and putting them to shame when they failed. Taniwha had never forgotten the dreadful day when Te Pou had found him crying, and had scornfully outlined the tears on his face with the bit of red ochre which he used for tracing his designs before he began to tattoo. The boy blushed with mortification at the very thought of it and he slunk past Te Pou's house hoping that the old man was asleep.

He had just turned his back and was sauntering on with a sigh of relief when a sharp resounding smack startled and stung him so much that his body described a curve, and he shot

through the gates and was outside the *pa* before
he knew that he had escaped.

Never had a slap from Te Pou been so unexpectedly welcome! Taniwha forgot how badly
the imprint of the artist's hand was smarting
and ran giggling into the woods. It was easy to
hide there, for the trees were overgrown with
parasitic plants and long snaky vines hung
down from the branches. For a long time the
little boy crouched among the ferns and shrubs,
peering through the tree tops at the darkening
sky. The moon was not yet up and Taniwha
wished it would hurry. He crept on hands and
knees in the undergrowth and stole a look at the
pa. No one was following. He could just see
the long thatched roof of Te Pou's hut, with
the fantastic red and yellow scroll work on the
lintels. The smoke-dried head of an enemy on
a high wooden stake was silhouetted against the
sky. A puff of wind caught a strand of the hair
and for a second the whole head wobbled.
Taniwha began to feel uncomfortable. He could
not see distinctly but he was sure the face was
grinning. Then he remembered gratefully that
the chief of the tribe had extracted the teeth
and used them as a necklace before fixing the
head above the gate, so perhaps it could not
grin.

He looked round. The woods were changing
colour. A faint silver sheen illumined the

leaves. The moon was up. Large, round and yellow, it floated from the horizon throwing a wide path of light on the sea. With bated breath Taniwha waited until the lower rim was well above the water. Then very solemnly he pulled down his eyelids, stuck out his underlip and said slowly and clearly: "Silly old tattoo-face!"

Nothing happened. Even Rona and her thorn-bush seemed very indistinct.

"Silly old tattoo-face!" said Taniwha again, grimacing hideously. "SILLY OLD TATTOO-FACE. SILLY OLD TATTOO-FACE!"

He looked down at his feet. They were still planted firmly on the ground.

"Silly old tattoo-face! Silly old ta——! Eeeeee!"

Something gave him a violent blow. His feet left the ground and he was jerked into the air.

"Silly old tattoo-face, eh?" said an angry voice and Taniwha found himself looking into the eyes of Te Pou. It was useless to explain that he had been addressing the moon and not the artist, and in any case when Te Pou was cuffing and shaking him the words would not come. Taniwha could only wriggle and grunt till the old man paused for breath, and then with a dexterous wrench he freed himself and ran home as fast as his trembling legs would carry him.

His brothers were asleep and his parents said nothing to the late comer, so he curled himself

"Silly old tattoo-face"

under a mat, closed his eyes and began to think. He had abused and made faces at the moon and she had taken no notice of him, so perhaps the story of Rona was untrue. Taniwha could not help being a little relieved. He felt his arms tenderly and pressed his tingling back against the soft mat. After all, the marks which Te Pou had left would not hurt for long and the moon's punishment might have lasted for ever. The thought comforted Taniwha and he fell asleep.

His adventure had tried him so that he slept heavily and awoke next morning later than usual. He rubbed his eyes and sat up. The room was empty. Bare feet were pattering excitedly up and down the verandah and there was a murmur of frightened voices. A woman cried, "Someone has offended the gods and they are going to punish us!"

Taniwha's heart leapt. He thought of the moon and peered anxiously through the door. The *pa*, which was usually quietly busy at this time of day, was in confusion. Two or three of the Maori warriors were standing on the lookout platform which towered nearly thirty feet above the roofs of the huts. They were shouting and pointing towards the sea. In the middle of the *pa*, the chief and some of the most important tribesmen were seated in council. They looked anxious and had evidently met hurriedly, for the chief had forgotten his carved staff and had not even put on his head-dress of kiwi feathers, while the others were wearing their common flax mantles instead of the soft feather cloaks which they always wore at a council. Women were talking in groups and some of the little girls were crying.

Taniwha ran across the verandah to some of his own friends, who were standing on tip-toe and lifting one another as high as they could. "What has happened?" he asked. "What are you looking at?"

All the little boys began to talk at once, pointing and gesticulating in the direction of the sea. "A flying monster, sent by the gods!" "A strange bird." "Great white wings!" "A baby bird beside it!" "So big, perhaps it will eat us."

Still thinking nervously of the moon, Taniwha stretched his neck and stood on tiptoe, but he could not see over the high palisade. "Come down to the beach," he cried and the others followed, running headlong through the *pa* till they came to Te Pou's house, where with one accord they turned and waddled sideways, keeping their backs well out of reach and their eyes fixed warily on the old man's door.

Once through the gate, they quickened their speed and sliding, scrambling, rolling, they stumbled helter-skelter down the cliff on to the beach below.

Taniwha shaded his eyes with his hands. "Oooh!" he gasped, "it's wings are as big as a house. And—and it's coming nearer. *Hide!*"

The boys darted behind some rocks, their little black heads peeping cautiously round the sides.

Taniwha was in great distress. If *only* his mother had not told him about Rona. It was all her fault. If he had not known that story he would never have insulted the moon and brought all this trouble. If only——!

"Eeee! A canoe."

Taniwha popped up from the rock like a rabbit. Then he squealed "There are goblins in it!" and with a terrified scuttle each black head ducked down again.

The strange white bird with its little one was now quite close to the shore, but the canoe, manned by goblins, was nearer still. Taniwha knew they were goblins because they seemed to have eyes at the backs of their heads, otherwise how could they know that they were paddling towards the shore? When a Maori was coming home in a canoe he paddled facing the land, so as to see where he was going. Taniwha groaned. He wished the moon were up, then he could apologise. He began to whisper, "Dear Moon! Pretty-face!" over and over again, until one of the boys pinched him and muttered angrily, "If they hear, they'll come and eat us."

By this time the goblins had beached their canoe and were wandering up and down, talking to one another in a hard hissing speech. Taniwha watched them anxiously. They looked so strange with their ugly three-cornered head-dresses and their arms, legs and bodies covered in such an uncomfortable way. Suddenly, one of them lifted a staff with a thin end and a thick top and pointed it at a cormorant which was sitting on a rock. There was a quick flash of lightning from the staff, a clap like thunder and the cormorant fell dead.

Screaming, "Goblins! Goblins with a magic stick!" all the little Maoris sprang from behind the rocks, scrambled up the cliff and fled, shrieking, into the woods.

Some time passed before they dared steal from their hiding-place and creep home to the *pa*. They were so glad to be back, that even the frowning face of old Te Pou held no terror for them. They scuttled through the dust eager to tell their families of this terrible adventure, when suddenly they stopped short, their jaws dropped and they stared at one another in open-eyed amazement.

There was the Maori chief in his kiwi head-dress and his best dogskin mantle lined with the minutest of blue, green and red feathers. There were the tribesmen, some in robes of woven flax with coloured borders and some in rough cloaks and waist-mats. There were the women, with their babies slung in cloaks on their backs, standing in a circle and silently staring. And there were the goblins sitting round a fire with the Maoris, talking, laughing and making the friendliest gestures.

The children took a few steps forward, and Taniwha, seeing his father in the group, walked straight up to the fire with a boldness which he was far from feeling. He squeaked with fright when one of the goblins tumbled him into the dust and began to tickle him. But he need not have minded, for the goblin soon set him on his feet, pulled his ear playfully and gave him three green beads.

The little boy was entranced. He wanted to eat the beads, but the goblin would not let him. Instead he shut them into Taniwha's hand, took the little boy on to his knee and began to talk. He tapped himself on the chest and said "Lieutenant Gore" three times, very distinctly. Taniwha looked solemn. At first he shook his head. Then he understood. Of course, that was the goblin's name. He tapped his own chest smartly. "Horeta Taniwha," he said.

The goblins repeated it and Taniwha was delighted. He ran round the circle, telling the names of the various tribesmen and trying to repeat those of the goblins. At last he came to the head of all the goblins. Taniwha knew he was the most important, because the others treated him with such deference, just as the Maoris treated their own chief. He felt a little shy, but went up to him and tapped him as respectfully as he could on the chest.

"James Cook!" smiled the goblin. "Cook."

Taniwha grinned. That was the easiest name which he had heard.

"Kuku," he said with his head on one side, and such a shout of laughter arose from all the goblins that Taniwha burst into tears and, with offended dignity expressed in every curve of his naked body, retired to his own hut, missing the fun which followed. And fun there certainly was, for the goblins began to trade with the Maoris, giving them nails, beads and looking-glasses for flax mats, and showing rolls of cloth to the women who fingered and stroked it with little coos of delight, willingly handing over their finest feather-lined mantles.

It was a shrill squealing mingled with loud grunts and snorts which lured the sulky Taniwha from his hut. The goblins had brought ashore the strangest little pink and black animals, which they called "pigs," and were letting them loose in the woods. Taniwha smacked his lips. He would get his father to take him hunting. He would spear those new animals just as he did the birds, and perhaps their flesh would taste as delicious as the little grey rats which his mother sometimes cooked for him.

The weeks which followed were full of excitement and although Taniwha soon made friends with the goblins, he had a wholesome fear of their magic walking-sticks and many days passed before he allowed himself to be taken in a canoe to visit the strange white bird. After all, he was only an ignorant little Maori and this was his first adventure. He had never heard of England. He did not know that there were other countries beyond the Long White Cloud. He knew no human beings but those of his own and the neighbouring tribes. He had never seen any boats but the Maori canoes, so how could he know that this strange white-winged bird and its little one were English sailing-ships, the *Endeavour* and her pinnace, which Lieutenant James Cook had brought on a voyage of discovery.

When Taniwha had lost his fear of the mysterious monster, he paid it many a visit and made friends with the sailors, eating their "salt junk" which nipped his throat till it brought tears to his eyes, learning how to climb ropes and row with his back to the land. Indeed, his life had become so amusing that he was quite sad when "Kuku" and the goblins bade him farewell and the great white-winged bird carried them out of sight. Taniwha stood on the shore and waved and waved until he could not even see a distant speck on the horizon.

"Gone!" he said and looked sadly at the *pa*, which seemed strangely dull.

"Gone," said the older Maoris, shaking their heads and wrinkling their tattooed foreheads, "but they'll come again."

They went back into the *pa*, and Taniwha saw them wrapped in their mantles holding a council with the chief. Then he strolled to his own hut, thinking so deeply that the whole of his face was puckered. He looked at the brass nail which he was wearing round his neck, at the three green beads and the tiny looking-glass. He thought of the white and scarlet cotton cloth, of the "salt junk" and the pig's flesh. Then he remembered the magic walking-sticks which had scolded and punished any rash youth who had tried to steal from the goblins.

Taniwha was puzzled. For a minute he stood quite still. Then he sighed, took up a mussel shell and began to make a fish-hook. He had resolved never again to make faces at the moon.

CHAPTER XII

THE BOSTON TEA PARTY

[A.D. 1773]

"Lobster! Lo—obster!" shouted the boys, jumping up and down and sending snowball after snowball at the discomfited English soldier, whose scarlet coat was bespattered with white flakes. He turned to shake his fist, but his black felt hat slid ignominiously over one eye, and the boys, punctuating their cries with snowballs, bombarded him.

"Taxation (plop) without representation (plop) is TYRANNY (plop, plop, plop)!"

Muttering something about "impident colonial warmints," the soldier savagely shook the branches of a snow-laden tree and broke off a switch, but he was too late. A final snowball knocked off his hat, and with a peal of laughter the boys sped down the road, sliding and falling along the slippery cart-tracks.

"And a good riddance," snorted the soldier. His pride was hurt. He did not mind being called a lobster, but the word "tyranny" had cut him to the quick. "Tyrants," he sniffed, "tyrants, indeed." He turned to the tree and hit it violently on the trunk. "And who," he demanded truculently, "defended 'em in the late war? Tyrants, ho." Still slashing at the trees, he strutted towards the castle with as much dignity as he could muster, but was startled by a snowball bursting on his left ear as another "warmint," shouting, "Go home, good dog!" tobogganed past him on a tea-tray.

A tin tray on a slippery hill makes a good sleigh, and Bob Andrews shot past the soldier and was out of reach before he could be caught. He giggled, shaking himself as he picked up the tray and shaded his eyes with his hands. The sun on the snow was dazzling and every tree sparkled. It was good to be alive on a crisp winter day and better still to be in Boston, where there was excitement in the very air. Bob gazed across the white distance to the harbour. He could just see the masts of a big sailing-ship and he grinned maliciously. Snugly tucked beneath her hatches that vessel carried the cause of all the excitement—a cargo of tea.

The merchants had declined to buy it. The housewives had joined a league and refused to drink it. The young girls had signed a document, saying "We, the daughters of those patriots who have appeared...for the public interest...do now with pleasure engage with them in denying ourselves the drinking of foreign tea."

Bob remembered how puzzled he had been when he had first heard about it, and how his elder brother in exasperation had pushed him

13-2

into the settle in the parlour and stood over him, saying "Don't you *see*, you little blockhead? Tea is taxed by the British government. There's an import duty on it. Well, taxation without representation is tyranny! England claims the right to tax her American colonies and we aren't represented in the English parliament. There-*fore*" (here he had knocked Bob's head against the back of the settle) "we don't intend to pay the tax or admit the tea. *Now* do you understand? Taxation without rep——." But Bob had fled.

He laughed as he thought of the episode and ruefully felt the back of his head, for he remembered the bumps, although they were several months old. With the tray under his arm and his high-crowned hat still powdered with snow, he strolled along the road and stopped before a poster which was nailed to the trunk of a tree. He had read the same notice in different parts of the town, but it never failed to give him a little thrill of excitement, so he stared at it, spelling the difficult words till he almost knew them by heart.

FRIENDS! BRETHREN!

COUNTRYMEN!

That worst of plagues, the detested tea shipped for this port by the East India Company, is now arrived in this harbour. The hour of destruction, of manly opposition to the machinations of tyranny stare you in the face. Every friend to his country, to himself and posterity, is now called upon to meet at Faneuil Hall, at nine o'clock, *this day*, at which time the bells will ring, to make a united and successful resistance to this last, worst and most destructive measure of administration.

Bob drew in his breath with a whistle and wondered what was going to happen. "This last, worst and most destructive measure of administration" puzzled him and he ran home, scuffling and sliding, to find his brother.

Dick was reading a news sheet in the parlour, and he gobbled like an angry turkey when Bob consulted him. "It's a trick," he said. "They're sending the tea straight from India. The route's shorter. The ships won't stop in England on the way, so they won't have to pay an export duty. I ask you" (he turned violently towards Bob), "*what does that mean?*"

Bob, keeping as far as possible from the settle, nervously admitted that he did not know, and Dick with a menacing glare flung out both arms and shouted: "It means that tea will be cheaper." As Bob appeared more mystified than ever, he banged his fists on the table and the large hairy mole on his wrist seemed to bristle with rage. "Tchah!" he cried irritably. "*Can't* you understand? If the company doesn't have to make such a long journey and doesn't have to pay export duty, they can afford to sell it at a lower price. I tell you it's a *trick*. The English government thinks that if we're given cheaper tea we shan't mind paying the tax. Shall we pay?" he thundered, advancing upon his small brother. And Bob, terrified of more bumps against the settle, stuttered breathlessly, "T—taxation without representation is t—tyranny." Whereupon Dick shook him solemnly by the hand, saying that nobody was too young to understand *this* situation, and began to talk of "patriotism" and "principles," while Bob, nodding his head sagely, thought that one day such a noble fellow would surely be a general.

He could not help feeling aggrieved when all the city bells began to clang and the noble fellow dashed off to the meeting, shouting with absurd inconsistency, "Go back. You're too young."

Bob stood in the doorway watching the wide skirts of his brother's coat swinging as he ran, and he swallowed his resentment as best he could. Peal after peal rang through the frosty air, and soon every street and by-way was filled with hurrying crowds. Men, muffled in thick coats with three-cornered hats on their heads, strode past in high boots or "frosts," which were provided with spikes on the soles to prevent them from slipping. Women, holding their full skirts above their ankles to keep them dry, scuffled along on pattens, and fashionable

ladies sat in sedan chairs with their chins uncomfortably bumping against their chests so
that their hair, rolled and dressed in towers at
least a foot high, need not touch the roof. In
the distance the "lobsters" were marching, two
and two, with shouldered arms. Hundreds of
people had come in from the country and Bob
saw many strangers, but he recognised his
father's old friend, Samuel Adams, who had
spoken with such eloquence at the indignation
meetings. Two other neighbours, Mr Rowe and
Mr Kent, hastened past him, swearing that not
a single pound of tea should be brought into
the town. Their powdered queues made untidy
white patches on their great-coats, and they were
talking so eagerly that they forgot the slippery
paths and were continually clutching one another to preserve their balance. Then Paul
Revere, with quick, lithe movements and steady
eyes, passed at a run. He grinned at Bob and
shouted "Look at Griffin's Wharf."

Naturally, Bob did not wait to be told twice.
Banging the door behind him, he ran upstairs
and leaned out of a window above the heads of
the crowd. He could still see the *Dartmouth*
lying at anchor, but she was no longer alone.
Two other ships were beside her. Bob recognised them as the *Eleanor* and the *Beaver*,
and he knew that they belonged to the East
India Company by their flags.

"They'll have to go back," he thought glee-
fully as he drummed his toes against the wain-
scoting. Then he stopped and stood quite still,
frowning a little and wondering how they would
pass the castle. He knew that men-o'-war prevented every ship, except the little coasters,
from leaving by any other route. He knew, too,
that no vessel was allowed to pass the castle
without a permit signed by the governor, and
a permit was never issued unless the ship had
been cleared at the customs, the duties collected and the goods landed. The only way to
prove that these rules had been obeyed was
to show a certificate called a "clearance"
signed by the collector and comptroller of
the customs. Bob scratched his head. If the
Bostonians were neither going to pay the duty
nor receive the tea, how could the ships be
cleared?

It was as puzzling as it was thrilling, and Bob
found it very difficult to wait patiently until
Dick returned with the news.

The big brother pushed his way into the hall
and stood at the foot of the stairs, shaking his
coat and stamping the snow from his feet. "Oh,
there you are," he said as he saw the small
figure a-quiver with excitement. "We refuse to
land the tea! The collector refuses to give a
clearance, and I'll stake my last coin that the
governor will refuse a permit for the ships to

return." Bob jumped up and down on the top stair, waving his handkerchief. "Hurrah," he shouted. "Hip, hip, hurrah! Stick-won't-beat-dog, dog-won't-bite-pig, pig-won't-get-over-the-stile, and we shan't get home to-night."

"Shan't we?" laughed Dick. "We'll get home to-morrow then. *And the tea will be cleared!*"

"Tell, oh *do* tell!" cried Bob. He scented a secret and paused with raised eyebrows, adding a disconsolate "Oh bother!" for Dick only smiled and said, "Wait till to-morrow," then walked upstairs and along the passage, looking important and mysterious.

Bob stumped after him and sat down to prepare his neglected lessons. But his mind was far away from sums and maps and, as he counted on his fingers, he thought wistfully that life always meant "waiting till to-morrow."

Even when "to-morrow" came, nobody seemed to want him. Dick disappeared early in the morning. In the afternoon his father, in a great-coat with a grey woollen scarf round his neck, walked grimly down to the old Meeting House. And his mother, wrapping a meat-pie and johnny-cake in a napkin, told him that she was going to be out all the evening, that he must go and play with his friends and be home before it was dark. She gave him the food and hid the key of the house under a loose stone in

the flagged path, and Bob found himself standing forlornly on the threshold.

He was not in the mood for play. He felt sure
that something unusual was happening and he
resented being treated like a child when he was
ten years old. After all, his brother had said
that no one was too young to understand the
situation, and instead of taking him to the
Meeting House, where the situation was obviously being discussed, they had told him to
go and play.

He began to scrape up the snow into a heap,
patting it with his hands to make it firm, but
although he was shaping quite a handsome
snowman, he was not thinking of what he was
doing. All the afternoon people were hurrying
past him. Sometimes they came singly, sometimes in couples and sometimes in large groups.
But they always went in the same direction. At
last, when the town clock struck five, Bob could
bear the suspense no longer. He kicked at the
snowman till it broke into three hard, dirty
lumps, thrust the napkin with the food deep
into his pocket and strode towards the old
Meeting House.

A large crowd was outside, but Bob stole
round to the back, cautiously opened the shutters,
scrambled on to the ledge and peered through
the window. In front stood Mr Rowe, talking
eagerly, quickly and with a glint of fire in his

eyes. Beside him sat Mr Samuel Adams, gravely attentive, with the thumb of one hand thrust into the arm-hole of his flowered waist-coat. The room was full. Every now and then an angry shout or an outburst of laughter greeted the speaker. Each bench, stool and chair was occupied. Men were sitting on the floor and standing against the walls. There was scarcely space for any movement. From his window Bob looked down on a sea of white faces which seemed to hover and sway in the dim candle-light.

The little boy pressed his ear to the window and listened.

"Gentlemen," said Mr Rowe, "who knows how tea will mingle with salt water?"

A loud cheer and a roar of laughter echoed through the room and the faces jerked back-wards and forwards. A sudden pause and a little scuffle announced a new-comer. Bob flattened his nose against the window and peered across the heads. Someone was trying to force his way to the front. He was using elbows and knees, and friendly hands were thrusting him forward. Bob recognised the strained, troubled face, and held his breath. It was Mr Rotch, the owner of the *Dartmouth*. He moistened his lips when he reached the front of the room. The silence was tense until somebody said "Well?" like a pistol-shot.

Then came the answer, slowly and clearly. "The Governor will not give a pass because the ship has not been cleared." He handed the governor's letter to Mr Adams who read it aloud.

For a few minutes everyone seemed to be talking at once and Bob could not distinguish the words. The white faces were distorted and the air torn with loud angry shouting. Then Samuel Adams rose to his feet. Immediately there was silence. Every eye was upon him.

He bowed. "Gentlemen," he said, "this meeting can do nothing more to save the country."

Then it was that Bob tumbled off the window-sill. He was startled by a blood-curdling yell, lost his balance and fell backwards on to the path. Of course he was bruised, but he picked himself up and ran round to the front of the house. He had heard a Red Indian war-cry.

At the porch of the old Meeting House the crowd was rocking with laughter. Dancing before the people, brandishing axes and hatchets, were some sixty Mohawks with feathers on their heads and blankets round their shoulders.

From highway, by-way, street and alley came men and women marching two and two towards Griffin's Wharf, and before them danced the Indians, leaping, circling and whooping—grim figures in the pale twilight.

Half-frightened, half-amused, Bob stared. He was so near to the Indians that he could almost touch them. Suddenly, he gasped. Their faces were copper-coloured but their arms and hands were white, and on the wrist of one there was a familiar hairy mole. Panting

Boston, in 1774

with laughter and the effort to keep pace with the crowd, Bob ran. At Griffin's Wharf somebody lifted him on to a little shed, and he sat clinging to the sloping roof and staring, bright-eyed and pale with excitement, as the "Indians" boarded the tea-ships.

Down came the axes and the hatches were broken. Up came the chests of tea on the backs of the yelling Mohawks.

"Throw it overboard," shouted the crowd.

"Whoo-oop, whoop!" yelled the Indians as they pitched the contents of each chest into the sea.

The blows of the hatchets, the splintering of the wood and the shouting drowned the steady lapping of the water against the wharf, but there was no disorder. Only once, the crowd grew angry and even Bob muttered "Traitor!" when someone ripped open the lining of his coat and waistcoat, filling them with tea. Bob cheered when the man's clothes were torn from his back and flung into the sea.

The little boy never knew how he managed to reach home. He had seen the contents of three hundred and forty chests flung into the waters of the harbour. He was bruised with jostling and hoarse with cheering, but somehow he must have struggled back to the house, for he found himself lying in bed, still wearing his boots and his great-coat.

The sound of a horse's hoofs had awakened him and he heard someone say: "It's Paul Revere, carrying despatches to New York." Then he stretched and sat up, yawning and rubbing his eyes, hardly noticing that his mother had begun to draw off his boots.

A candle was burning on the table and Dick was washing at the basin, an old red blanket on the floor at his feet and dribbles of copper-coloured water trickling down his neck.

"I suppose" said his mother softly, "this is the beginning of the end?" and she sighed, but Dick turned round harshly, scrubbing his neck with the corner of a towel.

"And whose fault is it?" he asked. "Why should they ask for dependence instead of a partnership?" He flung down the towel and strode across the room. "It means a break," he said.

Through half-closed eyes Bob saw that his mother looked wistful, but he was too sleepy even to kiss her, so he lay back on the pillows and began to float away into dreamland. From a long way off he heard his father's voice, "A break? Aye, but a break which will one day mean union,—union from South Carolina to New England."

CHAPTER XIII

MURADHANA OF KANDY

[A.D. 1815. The Final Conquest of Ceylon]

Muradhana lay on a low couch on the veranda, trying to think. His straight black hair was twisted into a tight knot at the back, and because he was resting he was not wearing the grand clothes of a chief's son, but a common sarong, wrapped round his waist and covering his legs but leaving the upper part of his brown body bare. Although he was only fourteen years old, a half-smoked cheroot lay on a plantain leaf beside him and his lips were scarlet from the betel which he was chewing. His brows were furrowed, and whenever the naked children of his father's household tumbled against his couch in their play, he frowned more fiercely and pushed them with his foot until they ran away, chattering like angry monkeys, with their bangles and anklets jingling.

Muradhana was anxious, for there was trouble in Kandy and he loved his native land. He stared across the hills. In the distance, Adam's Peak looked like a pointed shadow in the sky. Far below curled the unseen river winding its way through a tangled jungle, past the groves of rubber trees, where the birds never nested and the grass never grew, to a few scattered villages and bright green fields of rice. Hidden by his own hills and trees were the Sinhalese tea-plantations, where the Englishmen lived in little bungalows—the English, whose soldiers were making war upon Kandy.

Muradhana tossed restlessly from one side of his couch to the other. For two thousand years Kandy had been unconquered; for three hundred years she had resisted the attacks of Portuguese and Dutch, who were eager to win all the spices and perfumed woods of Ceylon; she had held her own against the English when every other Sinhalese had become a British subject, and now the white soldiers were marching nearer and nearer, and Molligode, the King's chief minister, had surrendered.

Muradhana thought of the King. Much had been happening in the palace by the lake, and it was hard to tell who loved and who hated Sri Vikrama Raja Sinha. There was Ehelapola, who had once been *adigar* or chief minister, a cunning ambitious man, who had rebelled, hoping to be King in Sri Vikrama's place. When he had been beaten in battle, he had fled like a coward to Colombo, fawning upon the English, betraying the secrets of Kandy. He had left his little sons at home, but because of his treachery, Sri Vikrama had seized and beheaded them, killing them in the presence of their mother, whom he had also slain. The

story had travelled the length and breadth of
the land, and all the chiefs and villagers had
been filled with horror, for to kill a woman was

Sri Vikrama Raja Sinha

against every law and tradition of Kandy. There
were some who said that the English would
make war on Sri Vikrama to avenge Ehelapola.
But nothing had happened, only the Kandyans
themselves had shrunk in disgust from their King.

Then came the day when some Kandyan villagers had wandered from their own hills towards Colombo. Along a deserted road they met a group of merchants with earthenware pots on their backs, reed baskets full of fish and bales of fine Indian muslin. Without stopping to think, they had set upon them, beating and robbing them. Then fearing punishment because the merchants were Sinhalese subjects of Britain, they had seized them and, driving them with blows and kicks to Kandy, had taken them before the King pretending that they were Ehelapola's spies. And Sri Vikrama Raja, nursing his rage against the treacherous *adigar*, had tortured the innocent merchants until seven had died and the others had crawled in pitiful agony back to Colombo.

It was then that the blow fell. British subjects had been injured. The governor of Ceylon declared war upon Kandy, and English soldiers forthwith marched into Kandyan territory.

It was whispered that some of the chiefs had begged them to come. Muradhana sat up wearily and spat the scarlet betel juice from his lips. His father Baddula Mudeliar was a strong partisan of Sri Vikrama, but the villagers were afraid of the English and had no love for the King, who had forced them to work for him, making them dig a great lake near his palace, until, weary with toil, their bodies had ached

and their spirits drooped. Muradhana wondered whether they would defend their homes
and fight for Sri Vikrama. He knew that other
villagers had fled to the jungle, deserting house
and shop, so that the English were marching
without trouble through a land which had always resisted the conqueror. The thought made
Muradhana square his shoulders. He looked
across the hills. He would fight till death for
Sri Vikrama Raja Sinha, because he was King
of Kandy.

The boy's thoughts were interrupted by the
sound of voices; he turned to see his father
coming towards him, followed by an old servant. The servant was shrugging his shoulders
and spreading his hands, and Muradhana could
see that the tears were pouring down his cheeks
as he hurried along beside his master.

Leaving the veranda the boy went to meet
them, but they shouted telling him to go back,
and for the first time in his life he saw the old
chief run.

"My son," said Baddula Mudeliar, "the
English are upon us. While I and my servants
defend the house, go you to the jungle with the
women and the children, that you may be safe
if the house be destroyed."

Muradhana tossed his head and shook off the
old servant, who had placed a pleading hand on
his shoulder. "I am fourteen, oh my father,"

he answered haughtily. "Am I a child or a woman that I should flee to the jungle? My place is at your side with sword and firearms."

He strode back to the veranda and stood proudly aloof, while his father called for all the women and children of his household and ordered them into the woods. His mother wept when she saw Muradhana, but he said nothing and remained standing as the women walked in Indian file towards the jungle, some with children sitting astride their shoulders and others with earthenware chatties of rice on their heads. For a few minutes he watched them, staring moodily, until their wailing died away into the silence of the jungle, and he saw that his father and the servants were fortifying the house.

The building was frail, but it was protected on three sides by mountains and forests, and it stood on a hill from which it was easy to attack an enemy. Only the front opposite the veranda was weak, for here the hill, sloping gently to the valley, was covered with rocks behind which the enemy could fight unseen.

Behind shelters made of furniture, logs and loose boulders, Baddula and his servants waited with their muskets across their knees. Muradhana was beside his father, eager to defend his home, but trembling partly from fear and partly from excitement. He could see the

English. Every now and then a helmet appeared above the rocks, and a sudden glimmer of light showed where the sun was flashing on the metal of a musket.

Baddula gave his orders. Ammunition was scarce. The Kandyans must fire only when they saw a helmet, and they must fire *without missing*.

The battle began. From their point of vantage on the hill the Kandyans could fight unscathed. They fired only when they saw a helmet, and they seldom missed their mark. But they were few in number, and slowly the English, under cover of the boulders, climbed nearer. For two hours this cautious fighting continued until about forty helmets suddenly appeared above the rocks, and with a wild cry the Kandyans levelled their guns.

Confused by the noise and dragged to his feet by his father and some servants, Muradhana found himself running towards the house, with Englishmen and Kandyans in a seething, struggling mass around him. Daggers, swords, the butt ends of muskets seemed to be whirling and beating on all sides, and before he knew where he was he was fighting like a wild beast on the veranda. He saw some of his father's men trampled underfoot as they fell wounded to the ground. He saw white-faced English soldiers carried away, bleeding. And then he saw his father fall.

He gave one terrified scream, while the little house, the friends and enemies seemed to be tumbling in a confused heap upon his head, and he knew nothing more until he found himself in an upper room, where two men were dressing his father's wounds.

"What happened?" asked Muradhana with his hands pressed to his aching brow.

"They put their helmets on their muskets," said someone, "then ran before we had time to reload. They were on the veranda as soon as we were. We just carried you and the chief upstairs in time."

"Where are they now?" whispered Muradhana, for he could not understand the sudden silence.

"They are below," answered one of the men. "Not even an Englishman would attack so narrow a staircase with an armed force above. We could pick off each one as he came."

Muradhana was silent, knowing that in spite of this encouraging reply, the house and all who were in it were in the power of the English. He looked at his father, who lay with closed eyes on the floor, scarcely breathing, then he stole across the room to the top of the staircase.

A group of Kandyans stood there with muskets levelled, and half-way down an old man, in the fine Indian muslin and silk robes of a chief, was stepping with measured tread. Muradhana could hear the plaintive voice: "I will give myself up if my people are unmolested."

Puzzled, the boy looked at his unconscious father and then at the stairs.

From the room below came the cool tones of the English officer, speaking Sinhalese in a strange clipped accent.

"I make no terms with rebels. Let Baddula be given up and the others may go where they will."

A quavering voice replied: "I am here."

From below came a murmuring, a slight scuffle, a cry "I did not promise to give up my son," and the curt answer, "I will not harm the boy, I merely wish to see him."

Puzzled and frowning, Muradhana looked first at his unconscious father and then at the staircase. Suddenly he laughed. The voice of his father's favourite servant called from below, "Muradhana, my son, come down." The boy leaned across the staircase. "*I understand*," he answered, and his voice was charged with meaning, "I am coming, father."

He ran down the stairs, burst through a group of English soldiers and throwing himself at the old servant's feet, cried "Oh father, father, they have put you in chains!"

The old man's eyes were full of grateful tears as he raised Muradhana.

The English officer nodded and strode to the

door. "Bring the prisoner," he said. "Let the boy go. Leave the others unmolested and fire the house."

With the faithful old servant between them, the English left the veranda and passed down the hill. For a minute Muradhana watched them, full of gratitude for the man who had pretended to be Baddula, but a smell of fire and the crackling of wood reminded him that his father was still unconscious in the burning building, and he fled up the stairs to help his comrades.

Carrying their wounded chief, the Kandyans left the flaming house and wound their way to the jungle. There they made a little shelter of leaves and branches, and they hid, nursing Baddula back to life.

But Muradhana brooded apart, heavy of heart and full of sorrow for Kandy. Day after day, he crept to the edge of the jungle and through the empty roads into deserted villages. Everywhere homes were abandoned, and gradually he learned that there had been so little defence that the English had marched into the capital city and, taking it almost unopposed, had captured Sri Vikrama Raja. Then Muradhana knew that Kandy was no longer a kingdom, that he would never again see Sri Vikrama Raja riding on the back of a royal elephant with his guards on each side and all the chiefs behind him.

At first the boy found it difficult to believe that Kandy had fallen, but scarcely three weeks passed before the fact was indelibly printed on his memory, for a day came when every chief was called to make submission and swear allegiance to the King of England.

Baddula Mudeliar was still too ill to move, but Muradhana dressed in his finest clothes, with a jewelled hat on his head and a jewelled girdle keeping his silk robes in place, went in his stead to the audience chamber in the palace.

Through a double line of English soldiers passed the Kandyan chiefs with Muradhana among them. The doors were flung open and there, at the end of the hall, where once the King of Kandy had received the ambassadors of Europe, sat the English governor, Sir Robert Brownrigg, in his laced uniform and gold epaulettes. The first to greet him was Ehelapola, who was given the place of honour at his right hand. Muradhana smiled bitterly when he saw the *adigar*. Was it through him that Kandy had been delivered to the enemy? The boy sighed as he walked up the hall, but he had little time to reflect, for when the governor had received each chief in turn, he stood up and in a loud voice made a proclamation.

Muradhana listened wistfully as the clear tones rang through the hall: "Led by the invitation of the chiefs and welcomed by the acclamation of the people, the forces of his Britannic Majesty have entered the Kandyan territory and penetrated to the capital.... The ruler of the interior provinces has fallen into their hands and the government remains at the disposal of His Majesty's representatives...."

Then a convention signed by the Kandyan chiefs was read, and while every British officer stood at attention and the Kandyans rose to their feet, King George III was proclaimed King over the whole of Ceylon.

Outside the cannon fired a royal salute and as the echoes rolled round the hills, the Union Jack was hoisted to the flag-post above the palace.

There was a moment's silence, then English officer and Kandyan chief talked together, greeting one another with ceremony and friendliness. But Muradhana slipped away. He strolled through the dusty roads and gazed over the hills. Everything looked the same. Acacias still drooped over the lake which Sri Vikrama had forced the villagers to build. Yellow-robed priests walked in the temple, where the holy tooth of the Buddha was enshrined in a jewelled casket, and the sacred turtles still swam in the moat. Cripples and beggars still grovelled at the temple gates, and one by one, girls in scarlet and gold walked down to the well, swinging their graceful hips, carrying their dark heads high and still, to balance their water-pots. On both sides of the road the little shops were selling painted chatties, fruit and vegetables, and on the ground coco-nut shells were drying. Under verandas thatched with plantain leaves men lay asleep and women sat combing their hair and spitting betel juice into the road. Jak and breadfruit grew in the jungle, the rice fields were as green as before, and down in the valleys men were tapping the rubber trees, or scrubbing the backs of buffaloes, which still wallowed in the grey mud.

Nothing had changed. But a red white and blue flag floated above the palace, and an independence, which had been maintained for two thousand three hundred years, had come to an end.

CHAPTER XIV

THE EMIGRANTS' JOURNEY

[A.D. 1819–20. The First British Settlers come to South Africa]

Susan, perching on the top of a large wicker trunk, looked like a bedraggled parakeet. The pink feather in her bonnet was out of curl and the hair underneath it, instead of hanging in neat brown ringlets on each side of the ruched tucker, fell in wet streaks across her face. There was a three-corner tear in her black apron, the colours in her check frock had run, a part of the braid had been ripped off and was hanging in a loop, while the new-fashioned *pantalettes*, of which she had been so proud, were clinging to her legs like grimy stove-pipes, all bespattered with wet sand. To add to her troubles, a rude boy lounged beside her, giggling and singing "Polly Flinders" with an obvious appreciation of the last three lines.

Taking no notice of her tormentor, Susan glowered at the unconscious back of a soldier in the Twenty-First Light Dragoons, and muttered "Pig!" under her breath. He was the cause of her mortification and her cheeks flamed when she thought of him. She looked about her dolefully. If these were the joys of emigration, she wished that she had stayed at home.

At first, everything had been interesting and

new. Susan had not minded the discomforts on board the crowded *Chapman*, for whenever anything disagreeable had happened, the corners of Mamma's mouth had suddenly twitched into a smile and, although her eyes sometimes filled with tears, she always hugged Susan and said, "Isn't this an *adventure?*" till the child had begun to feel that she was living in a story-book.

For instance, there was that exciting arrival at Deptford, where all the emigrants were waiting in the snow surrounded by bundles and boxes and great piles of bedding, sown up in brown sacking with stitches of string instead of cotton; then the funny little cabin on the *Chapman* like a black cupboard, with no beds, no chairs and not even a basin to wash in, only two bunks like shelves on the wall covered with straw mattresses and a couple of thin blankets. The voyage through the Channel had been the worst part, for even Mamma had looked very white and miserable, and poor Susan, unable to touch the food, which smelt of bilge-water, and terrified of wind and waves, had been so sea-sick that she had temporarily lost all affection for Papa, who would insist upon waking her just as she was beginning to doze, by bouncing into the cabin and being cheery. This, however, had not lasted for long, and Susan had really enjoyed the four months in the Atlantic Ocean when she had played at ball with wet sand-bags, learned how to throw quoits on to a wooden peg and sung songs with the other children, while Mr Baillie, the gentleman in charge of the party, had picked out the accompaniments on his guitar. The food, too, had been plentiful though rough, and although Susan grew tired of salt-junk and hard ship's biscuits, she was given a liberal supply of tea, sugar, coffee and cocoa and three quarts of fresh water every day. Sometimes the steward's wife brought Mamma a fresh egg, for the *Chapman* carried poultry, which the little girl loved to feed when the sailors were in a good temper and would take her to see them.

She became quite fond of one sailor, for he was always ready to tell stories, and Susan never forgot his description of the sheep at Cape Colony. "Tails, they have, as thick as both my legs together," said he, "and no wonder. You see, missy, they graze on the slopes of Table Mountain, with their heads always towards the top and so, quite natural-like, the fat slips down to their tails."

It was the arrival at Algoa Bay which had distressed the child. In spite of the broad belt of angry breakers which lashed the shore, the sandy landscape with its tussocks of coarse grass and the Winterhoek Mountains looking like a gloomy cloud in the sky, she had joined in three lusty cheers when the *Chapman* had lowered her anchor. It was a great adventure to scramble down a rope-ladder into one of the flat-bottomed surf-boats which were waiting to take the emigrants ashore, and Susan shouted with excitement when the men of the Twenty-First Light Dragoons came wading towards them, bare-legged and with their trousers pulled up above their knees. One by one they had picked up the emigrants and carried them. Fat and thin, great and small were seized without ceremony and conveyed, laughing and screaming, through the shallows to dry land. There was Papa riding pick-a-back on a tall dragoon and Mamma with her arm round a soldier's neck, looking something like an overgrown long-clothes baby, with her velvet bonnet awry and her brown ringlets bobbing up and down as though they were on springs. Susan had jumped about till the surf-boat rocked, begging her soldier to race them and he had winked and said "Certainly, missy. Father of a family, I am. Know what's what." Then, to the little girl's horror, he had grabbed her by the apron-strings and instead of swinging her to his shoulder where she would have been quite dry, he shouted "'Ere, mates, give us a little 'un to balance," seized another small girl, tucked one under each arm as though they had been sacks of flour, and rollicked through the surf, splashing in all directions while the tips of their little cross-over sandals and the hems of their frocks dipped in the water, and all their petticoats were hitched up behind, leaving their legs dangling so helplessly that everyone roared with laughter. To make matters worse, the soldier too seemed to think it amusing, and before setting the children on their feet he danced a few steps of the hornpipe, then, smoothing their clothes with a grimy hand, he chucked them both under the chin, saying "Got two such poppets of me own at 'ome," and sauntered off, unaware that he had ruffled their dignity even more than their petticoats.

"Pig, *horrid* pig," said Susan again. Her voice was husky and she tried to wet her finger and rub away some of the smears on her frock, choking when she thought of the parlour at home with the neat muslin curtains and the pots of musk in the window, where the neighbours had met to bid them good-bye. They had said, "What a lucky little girl," when they saw Susan's new clothes, and she had felt happy and excited. But now England, the kind neighbours and the clean little brick house seemed very far away from Cape Colony, and Susan looked around disconsolately.

It was all noise, bustle and confusion. People were shouting and dragging boxes across the sand, giving them impatient jerks when they stuck against the hummocks of grass. Some of the soldiers were standing at attention while a blue-coated officer, with beads of perspiration running down his forehead, was rapidly giving them orders. Mounds of agricultural implements lay under tarpaulins on the beach. Packing cases and bundles of every shape and size littered the foreground, and for some five or six hundred yards the landscape was made hideous by tottering heaps of tins and wooden boxes. On the slopes behind Susan evergreen bushes were growing among the sandhills, but they were hidden by two or three large marquees, some cabins roughly built of logs and several rows of small tents pitched closely together. On a tree at one side somebody had nailed a board on which the words "SETTLERS' CITY" were printed in straggling letters of white chalk.

Susan sniffed. "People over here seem to have strange ideas of a city," she thought, staring wearily at the untidy muddle. A tear crept from the corner of her eye, rolled down her cheek and dropped with a tiny splash on the back of her hand. She swallowed, knowing that in two minutes she would be crying in earnest, when a cheerful voice behind said "A penny for your thoughts, little Patience-on-a-monument," and there was Mamma with a clean apron protecting her skirt and laughter written all over her face.

Susan felt ashamed when she confessed her thoughts, but Mamma said very little, only smiled and squeezed her hand as they picked their way among ropes and pegs to their own tent. "When English people are together, England need never seem far away," she said. "Don't you think that it's wonderful to bring a little bit of England all the way to South Africa?"

Then she talked to Susan of the new home which they were going to have, and how the government was giving them many acres of land rent-free for three years, after which they would have title-deeds to show that they owned the land and would only have to pay a small quit-rent. She drew such a fascinating picture of the little town which the emigrants were going to build, and of the pride which they must take in making it beautiful and useful, that Susan began to feel excited again. Then she laughed and hugged the little girl. "Why, poppet," she said, "instead of building houses on the parlour floor with blocks or cards, you'll help Papa to make a real house, and we'll all live in it to-gether. Dear me, we seem to be in the wrong row." She paused, puzzled, then drew Susan down another alley of tents where flustered parents were alternately scolding and petting their children and everything seemed to be squalid and untidy. Through the open flaps Susan could see the emigrants moving about eating, washing and unpacking their bundles. There were weather-beaten fishermen from the English sea-ports, groups of pale-faced artisans and factory hands from the northern counties, tradesmen who must have seen better days and jolly red-faced farmers who were laughing at one another, shrugging their shoulders and saying "Here's pasture for you! Hummocks of coarse grass and miles of sandhills. Well, well!" Some women grimaced sympathetically at Mamma as she led Susan into the tent. "Ours are in just such a pickle," they said, "and we haven't a clean petticoat or pair of trousers between them!"

But Susan did not care. She had forgotten the torn pantalettes and her undignified entry into Cape Colony. She could think of nothing but helping to build a real house, and so, rolled in a rug, she fell happily asleep to a confused murmur of voices, the barking of dogs and the thrum-thrum-thrum of Mr Baillie's guitar.

As the tents were needed for new arrivals, who were following on the other emigrant ships, Mr Baillie did not allow his party to remain for long at Algoa Bay. Within a few days he had taken to the road, and once again the ninety

men, fifty-eight women and a hundred and
eight children continued their journey.

To Susan, who had never travelled by road in
anything but a stage-coach driven by a drags-
man in a beaver hat and a coat with three little
capes, the journey was like a fantastic dream, for

Travelling in South Africa

along the rough tracks which led through the
open veldt and up the steep hills trundled
ninety-one ox-waggons. Each had a span of
twelve or fourteen oxen, driven by bearded
Dutchmen who shouted and grumbled in a
foreign language, cracking their long whips
and screaming at the naked Hottentots who led
the foremost oxen. Some of the waggons were

covered with canvas tilts and some were open and piled high with luggage, which was swept off by the branches of the trees as the oxen plodded slowly through the bush.

Never before had Susan walked till her legs ached. Never had she sat so uncomfortably on a mound of luggage, jogging and shaking from low to high ground, past stretches of desolate country where the distant mountains and impenetrable bush filled her heart with fear. Never before had she crossed a river, clinging to her Papa's arm while the water passed over the wheels of the waggon and some of the goods fell and were carried away by the current.

Day after day the journey continued, at first parallel to the sea, but afterwards out of sight of the ship—the one thing which seemed to link them to England—over flat country, through steep bushy roads, up barren and wooded heights, through the inhospitable Karoo, and across the drifts. Night after night Susan slept in a tent or on a rug within sight of Mamma, who sat by the other women round the camp-fire with her skirt turned back across her knees and the shadows from the flames dancing about on her white stockings. Morning after morning there was the dressing, without washing or after a cold sponge in river-water, the cooking of breakfast over a camp-fire and the interminable hunt for the oxen, which had been loosed over-night and had wandered into the thickets.

As the time passed, Susan began to think that they were never going to arrive, and one day she grew so tired of asking "When shall we be there?" and of hearing Mamma's "Very soon" and Papa's irritable "Hush, Susan, children should be seen and not heard!" that she curled up on a basket and went to sleep.

Dreaming that she was driving in an old stage-coach drawn by Hottentots, she awoke considerably later with a start just as the ox-waggon gave a lurch and came to a standstill. Rubbing her eyes and yawning, she peered under the canvas tilt and saw that all the waggons had stopped, while the emigrants were busily unloading their goods and pitching tents. At the door of her waggon she heard Mr Baillie talking to Papa. "Yes," he was saying, "this is the great Fish River and here are the locations which the government has measured for us." His voice sounded tired and despondent. Susan could not hear Papa's answer, but she caught the words "industry" and "determination," as she scrambled out of the waggon to look at her future home.

It seemed to the little girl that she had passed, as though by magic, into a new country. The Karoo had disappeared. The ground was no longer flat and arid, but watered by a beautiful river. Mimosa trees with feathery branches drooped over the fresh green grass. The hills looked friendly and the wooded valleys and meadows fertile. The land was almost like a park, but her heart sank a little when she saw how quickly the Dutchmen unloaded the waggons, and with a pitying "good-day" drove back towards Algoa Bay, leaving the emigrants with no shelter but the blue sky and a few tents borrowed from the government.

The journey was over, but the settler's life had begun.

It would take a long time to describe the difficulties and pleasures of those early days, the friendships and the quarrels; how some people wept from sheer misery, turned their backs on the "locations" and went away; how others worked till their heads and limbs ached, lending each other a helping hand and sleeping under the open sky.

Susan, like the other children, was sometimes fretful and sometimes gay. When Papa had prepared a small piece of land, she helped Mamma to plant and grow vegetables. Sometimes she went on a long, tiring journey to buy tea or coffee, sugar, candles, and soap from a central store, which the government had established within reach of the different locations. Sometimes she went to meet Papa to help him drive back the sheep which the government supplied as rations. If he and the other men were bringing sacks of flour on their backs, she and Mamma would drive to the river in an ox-waggon, waiting till they had waded safely across and then relieving them of their burdens.

The building of homes was weary work, for there were at first no planks. Some people simply dug themselves holes, where they lived under a covering of canvas. Others filled up the spaces between rocks and so had some sort of shelter. But Papa built Mamma and Susan a real house. It was only made of wattle and daub but it had two rooms, each about twelve feet square and ten feet high. A rug was hung across the entrance and an old white apron nailed in the window as a blind. It was rough and uncomfortable, but Susan was proud of it for she had helped to collect the rushes and grasses for the thatch.

All her life she remembered the day when that house was finished and how Papa carried Mamma across the threshold for luck. But there was another day which made an even greater impression on her. That was November 9th, 1820.

For weeks she and the other children had gathered together, talking of the treat which was in store for them, and when at last the great day dawned, they were almost too excited to be patient. Dressed in their best clothes, which had been packed away since they left England, the little people danced round the grown-ups, chattering, laughing, asking endless questions, and of course getting in everyone's way, until at last, some walking, some driving, they set out on a journey.

To a tune of her own Susan was singing "We're going to see the foundation-stone laid! Hurrah, hurrah! A real settlers' ci—ity. Hurrah, hurrah!" till the grown-ups cried "For mercy's sake, child! You'll frighten the oxen." But Susan could hardly keep still. She knew that a fine piece of land had been chosen to the east of Kowie River and eight miles from the sea, that surveyors had been busily dividing and marking it for public buildings and that already a British magistrate was there in a marquee, ready to help the emigrants in their troubles and to keep law and order in the locations. She knew that a real city was going to be built within reach of the little daub huts and vegetable plantations.

Her heart beat triumphantly, and as she jogged along in the waggon she saw settlers from many distant locations journeying in the same direction. They waved and cheered. "Going to Bathurst?" they shouted and laughed. But Susan did not laugh. She gave Mamma a sudden hug. Bathurst was a link with England, for it was the name of the Secretary of State.

To Susan the ceremony was the most wonderful thing that she had ever seen. From far and near the settlers had journeyed through the bush to see the birth of their city. Men, women and children, in clothes ragged or fine, crowded round the marquee and gave three ringing cheers when the commander of the frontier led his wife to the triangle on which the foundation-stone was suspended. When she saw him in his brilliant uniform with his medals shining, Susan thought that the King could not be finer, and of course she could not take her eyes off the lady. How she coveted the poke bonnet and the little tucked frill inside it, the embroidered shawl with its heavy fringe and the full blue skirt, high-waisted and garnished with a ribbon which crossed below the breast. The little girl stared with admiration. Then she clasped her hands and nearly closed her eyes with excitement, for the lady pulled a chain and the foundation-stone was lowered slowly to the ground.

There followed loud cheers, a sumptuous dinner, and the friendliest of talks with settlers from all the different locations, and it was a very sleepy Susan who travelled home in the ox-waggon that evening.

"Well, Susan," said Mamma, "is England still so far away?"

The little girl smiled drowsily. Her face was thoughtful but happy. She knew that she was thousands of miles away from her native land, but when she looked back at the marquee and saw the tall magistrate standing there in his military uniform, she felt that she was still under the care of the British government. And when she remembered the foundation-stone of Bathurst, her eyes were bright with dreams of the future, for she was sure that one day the beautiful new land would have cities as fine as those which she had left behind in the old country.

CHAPTER XV

IN THE BLACKFELLOWS' CAMP

[A.D. 1835. John Batman helps to found Victoria in Australia]

The clouds, hanging low in the sky, hid the morning star, and the camp was in darkness except for the faint red glow of some dying embers which illumined the nearest mia-mia. Under this rough shelter of bark and boughs Latingata's parents were asleep, with the baby still lying on its mother's breast and Banganoo, the little brother, rolled in an opossum-skin cloak at her feet. Only Latingata was awake, and she lay on her side with her head propped on her hand and her black eyes staring into the darkness. She was listening intently for some sound which was to come from the bush. Close beside her, she could hear the snuffling sighs of the dingos, asleep by the fire, with their heads between their yellow paws and the white tips of their tails stretched straight behind them. From the other mia-mias came the grunts and deep breathing of the blackfellows enjoying the heavy rest of hunters, weary with stalking kangaroo, wombat and wallaby. Behind these familiar sounds she caught the whisper of the bush, the flutter of leaves as the wind passed through the gum trees and the rustle of the tall grass, faintly stirred. But she was waiting for something else, and as she listened, motionless, nature seemed to turn in her sleep with a long deep sigh and in the bush something laughed. At first it was the ghost of a chuckle, but gradually it grew louder, until at last it became a long, hysterical cachinnation and the bush rang with peal after peal of discordant mirth.

Latingata sat up and pushed her wavy black hair out of her eyes. The coocooburrah (laughing jackass) was the herald of dawn and the sound of his voice was welcome, for Latingata was hungry and had planned an early expedition with Banganoo to dig for yams and those juicy white grubs which fed upon the rotten roots of trees and made so sweet a breakfast. She pushed the little boy with her foot and he rolled on to his back with a grunt, then sat up and listened. Satisfied that the coocooburrah had begun to call, he picked up his dilly-bag and trotted after Latingata.

Neither child would have stirred before daylight, for each was afraid of the devils and sprites which came out at night seeking for honeycombs and lily flowers. They knew that the coocooburrah was the friend who foretold the rising of the sun. Long ago Biami, the creator, and the good spirits who lived above the sky had asked him to be their messenger and he had agreed. Banganoo and Latingata knew the whole story, although it had happened thousands of years earlier, when there were no men at all, and only birds and beasts roamed the earth and spirits lived in the sky. In those days, the whole world was dark except when the stars came out, yet the beasts and the birds must have been able to see one another, for once when Dinewan (the emu) and Bralgāh (the crane) were quarrelling, Bralgāh flew into Dinewan's nest, seized one of her great eggs and threw it into the sky. Up in the sky Biami and the other good spirits kept a pile of wood. The egg fell into it and broke, so that the yolk splashed all over the logs, and suddenly a yellow flame leaped up and consumed them. The glow from the fire lighted the face of the world, and all the birds and beasts looked up and marvelled at the warmth and beauty. When Biami saw how pretty the earth looked under this rosy light, he was determined to make a fire every day, and he bade the spirits collect a huge pile of wood by night and set it alight in the early morning. So that the birds and the beasts, the trees and the flowers and all the rivers, hills and rocks should know when it was time for the fire to be lighted, Biami sent the Morning Star as a messenger. But in the early morning the world slept soundly, and the pale glow of the star could wake neither bird nor beast. "We must find someone who will make a great noise," said Biami, and as he spoke he heard from the earth below the shrill harsh cry of the coocooburrah. "We will ask him to be our messenger," said Biami. "If he refuses, we will trouble no further. The fire shall go out and the earth remain as dark and cold as before." The coocooburrah, who loved the warm light, readily agreed to help Biami. And so, year after year, in the still small hours when the light of the Morning Star was growing dim, he lifted his voice and woke the world, warning everyone that a new day had dawned.

Banganoo and Latingata never dared to imitate his mocking laugh lest he should be offended. They knew that if he refused to give his message Biami and the spirits would never again light their bonfire, and the world would grow cold and dark.

As they strolled through the bush with their yamsticks, the children looked up. The fire was evidently burning well, for the sky was growing brighter and there was a rosy light on the silver trunks of the gum trees. In a few minutes they found a clear space and began to dig in the ground, spearing tubers and roots with their sticks and picking things up as easily with their toes as with their hands. They wanted as many provisions as possible for themselves as well as for the camp, so they shook out the contents of their dilly-bags and began to repack them in order to make room for the yams.

Both bags were made of grass and held the children's treasures. Banganoo had some bone fish-hooks and a long piece of twine skilfully woven from the fur of a bandicoot. He had a boomerang, like his father's in shape but smaller and lighter. He could swing it round his head just as the hunters did, and make it whirl through the air for a long distance and return almost to his feet. He had a little stone axe, too, and many a time he used it for cutting notches in the bark of a tree, so that he could climb and pretend to pull an opossum out of its hole. He was not quite old enough really to catch an opossum, but he was skilled in tracking the animal, and if he examined a tree trunk carefully he knew which scratches on the bark were made by its claws, whether they were fresh or not, and whether the creature had been climbing up or down. He had also some little stone balls in his dilly-bag. They were toys which he and the other boys held between their fore and middle fingers, making them spin on a smooth piece of bark.

There were no toys in Latingata's bag. She was older than Banganoo, and because she was a girl she led a busy life in the camp and carried things which were useful in everyday life. She had needles made from the shin-bone of a kangaroo and animals' sinews to sew with, a fresh-water mussel shell for scraping yams and for cutting her hair, a round stone for pounding, a precious lump of beeswax for greasing her body, and a cake of gum, carefully wrapped in a piece of bark and tied with some dried grass stalks. She had two *banksia* cones and a bit of dried fungus to help a fire to burn brightly, a piece of bark, cup-shaped, for carrying water, and the shavings of some kangaroo skins which were useful for polishing. Had she been grown-up she would have carried pipe-clay and red and yellow ochre for painting her body, and possibly a necklace made of beads cut from the stem of a reed, or of kangaroo teeth, but she would not begin to paint and decorate her body until she was old enough to be married, just as Banganoo would keep all his front teeth until he attained manhood, when he would undergo the sacred ceremony of initiation and the middle tooth would be knocked out with a stone.

Latingata and her brother packed their treasures carefully, tucking the yams into the corners of the dilly-bags and wrapping the largest white grubs in bits of bark. They were kneeling, absorbed in their task, when a faint "Cooee" came from the distance, and with an exclamation both children leaped to their feet and ran. Someone was warning all who had strayed from their homes to return.

Hopping and running through the bush, Banganoo and Latingata arrived to find everyone wide awake and the camp humming with excitement. The mia-mias were empty and the fires, which had sunk so low during the night, were burning brightly. Young women, with

Mother and Child

babies slung in bags on their backs, were roasting roots on the ends of pointed sticks, nodding at one another and throwing quick looks over their shoulders towards the outskirts of the camp. The old women were sitting cross-legged in a circle, talking in shrill, high-pitched tones, gesticulating with hands like claws and wrinkling their wizened faces until their eyes seemed to disappear. They were almost naked, but the skin cloaks which hung from their shoulders down their backs made them look like a number of old opossums sitting in council. Only one woman knelt apart, pounding the roots of a tree fern with a stone, and every now and then uttering a long wailing cry. Her face was daubed with white clay and her hair matted with gypsum so that it hung in long white sausages over her cheeks and neck. Banganoo and Latingata passed her with averted faces. The white paint showed that she was in trouble. The dead body of her baby was still in the mia-mia and they knew that she wanted to be alone until she was out of mourning, when she would cease to wail and cut her body with mussel shells, and would go about with the other women, without the hideous white clay on her face and hair and with the bones of her little baby carefully packed in her dilly-bag. The children scarcely gave her a thought, but ran to the middle of the camp where they had seen a little crowd, and there, with a group of old men and warriors before him, sat the "dreamer," a thin grey-bearded blackfellow with a long bone thrust through his nose. All the men and women of the tribe consulted him in their difficulties. Even the wise medicine-man, who could cure pain and disease by charms as well as by herbs, was known to visit his mia-mia and talk in hoarse anxious whispers, for the dreamer understood magic too. He could fore-tell the future by signs which he saw in his sleep, and in his dilly-bag he kept stones and sticks which could work untold harm on an enemy. He had been dreaming, and now every man in the tribe was eager to hear his pro-phecies. The two children edged closer and listened, but he spoke very little, and jerking his head from left to right, pointed to the edge of the camp, saying "He has come."

Banganoo and Latingata followed his finger and stood still, staring. Through the gum and wattle trees at a short distance from themselves sat a motionless figure. It was a blackfellow, but he had evidently come from another part of the country, for he wore no covering but a belt made from the skin of a wallaby, into which he had thrust his boomerang and throwing-stick. He was holding no weapons, but was gazing fixedly at the camp with one hand in his lap and the other stretched stiffly before him. To make his presence known he had lighted a small fire of bark and twigs, and the children saw with relief that he had brought a friendly greeting, for the hand which was pointing towards the camp held a flat red message-stick. Had he brought bad news or a challenge, the stick would have been painted white and, instead of talking to the dreamer, all the warriors of the tribe would have been busily pointing their spears.

While Banganoo and Latingata were watching, one of the old men left the camp. He carried a burning branch in his hand, and as he walked towards the stranger the smoke floated behind him in a long quivering line. For a few minutes he stood still, gazing in silence. Then he spoke to the messenger, received his token and conducted him to the camp. The two children strolled after them, curious to know the news and watching with eyes half-closed. When they heard that visitors were coming before sunset, bringing a white man, they scuttled like two startled bandicoots to their own miamia, calling to their mother in tones as shrill as those of the little green parrots which fluttered from bough to bough in the sunshine.

As the news flew from lip to lip, the camp became more and more like a hive of bees. The old people gathered about the messenger talking. The hunters seized their throwing-sticks and walked with wary noiseless tread into the bush. Children—armed with baskets made of bark, and yamsticks—ran to collect roots and firewood, while all the women bustled hither and thither making preparations for a feast.

Banganoo drew in his breath and sniffed the

air luxuriously. He enjoyed the smell of roast meat and his eyes sparkled when he saw his mother throw an opossum on to the fire, then pull it out and tear off its wool before roasting it in the hot embers. She gave him a scrap of meat to suck when it was ready, but he had to be content with a very small piece and he would not even share it with Latingata who came up to him licking her lips. He pushed her in the stomach with his elbow and she screamed at him, dancing up and down with quick angry steps, but he did not care. He finished the meat and she had to go back to her work. For a long time he watched her digging a large hole while the tears ran down her cheeks, leaving tiny pale rivulets in the dirt which caked her skin.

The day seemed to pass very quickly, and Latingata's hole was only just ready when the hunters returned with their prey. Slung on the strong branch of a tree by its feet, which were tied together with twine made of human hair, was the body of a kangaroo. As soon as they saw it, the women, grinning and chattering with delight, filled Latingata's hole with hot stones which they covered with grass; then with a shout of joy they lowered the body of the kangaroo and, piling a mound of earth above it, left it to roast slowly. They were satisfied that the strangers would have plenty to eat.

Banganoo and Latingata sat by the oven with

large skin bags full of water at their sides. It was their duty to make holes in the earth covering and pour in the water so that there should be sufficient steam in which to cook the kangaroo. The pleasant smell made Latingata forget her quarrel over the opossum meat, and she chattered to Banganoo, joyfully anticipating the feast and the corroboree which was sure to follow. The children had never seen a white man, although they knew that if they were to journey east and west through the bush and over the uplands, they would reach the "camps" of the white folk and see their high wooden miamias, the strange seeds which they had sown and the animals which they pastured in the grasslands. The idea that there were millions of such people in another part of the world never entered their heads, for they were only untutored little savages, who scarcely thought of anything but the food which they were to eat or the task with which they happened to be busy.

The sound of some sticks breaking, and the excited squawking of a parrot disturbed by an unwonted noise, warned them that the strangers were near, and they looked up to see one white man walking towards the camp with a train of blackfellows behind him.

The visitor did not come with a lighted stick in his hands according to the custom of the blackfellows, but he walked up to the eight chief tribesmen and shook hands, smiling. Then he sat upon the fallen trunk of a tree with his servants around him and the tribe proceeded to welcome him. Stretching out their arms north, south, east and west, they welcomed him to the forest lands. Cutting boughs from gum, wattle and *banksia*, they welcomed each guest to the trees, and spreading grass and leaves in green heaps at their feet, they welcomed them to the herbs which grew in forest and pasture. At last as a sign of friendship they brought them water to drink, stirring it with a reed and tasting it first to show that it was fresh and harmless.

Banganoo and Latingata were well used to these ceremonies, and they were not surprised when the white man sat in council with the chiefs. But they looked at his attendant black-fellows with awe. These men were of their own race but not of their tribe. They lived near the white men's camps and had learned how to speak their language. Some of them were talking now, explaining to the chiefs what the white man was saying, and the tribesmen were nodding their heads, a little puzzled but apparently agreeing. Presently the children saw the eight chiefs and their visitor leave the camp, and going up to a tree make a mark upon it with an axe.

On his return the white man seemed very much pleased. He laughed and talked, chucked

the black children under their chins, and
pinched Banganoo's cheek till the little boy's
face tingled. Then he clapped his hands, and at
that moment the most amazing thing happened.

The blackfellows, who had come with the
stranger, gathered about him and spread at his
feet several immense bundles. Banganoo and
Latingata gazed in solemn silence as the ropes
were untied and out of the bundles fell a cascade
of things which they had never seen before.
There were glass beads, knives made of steel
instead of stone, scissors and looking-glasses,
blankets softer than the skin of any animal, and
hatchets so sharp that they would sever a log at
one blow. There was something for everyone,
and the eight chiefs who had talked with the
stranger grinned from ear to ear as they loaded
their wives with their new possessions.

Banganoo and Latingata were made so happy
with a knife and a small mirror that they almost forgot the feast, and only came to their
senses when the smell of burned fur and roast
meat began to tickle their nostrils. When the
strangers had been served, the children fell
upon the scraps which were left, tearing the
meat with their teeth, and splitting the bones
so as to pull out the marrow. To Latingata, the
corroboree which followed the feast was far
the most amusing part of the day, and she
beamed with delight as the blackfellows, with

painted faces and coloured feathers in their hair, danced backwards and forwards brandishing their boomerangs. The little girl sat in the circle of women, copying their actions and joining the chorus of their voices. Across her

The Corroboree

knees an opossum skin was stretched taut and she beat time on it, singing in a raucous squeal:

The frogs in our pool are *good* frogs!
The frogs in our pool are *good* frogs!
The frogs in our pool are *good* frogs!

over and over again to preserve the rhythm of the dance.

Banganoo watched for a short while, but for the first time in his life he was not interested in the corroboree. His eyes strayed to the white man who seemed to be drawing. Banganoo had often seen his father making the figures of animals on bark, and he wondered whether the stranger were as clever. He stole from the others and peeped over the white man's shoulder, putting his head first on one side and then on the other, but he could not understand the picture. Thinking that the visitor was making his own sacred mark like the chiefs of every tribe, the child slipped away, little knowing that the white man was merely writing in his diary:

I purchased two large blocks or tracts of land about six hundred thousand acres and in consideration thereof gave blankets, knives, looking-glasses, tomahawks, beads, scissors, flour, etc. Also I further agreed to pay a tribute or rent yearly. The parchment was signed by the eight chiefs, each of them, at the same time, handing me a portion of the soil; thus giving me full possession of the tracts of land I had purchased. This most extraordinary sale and purchase took place by the side of a lovely stream of water from whence my land commenced. A tree was here marked to define the corner boundaries....

Had he been able to read, Banganoo would not have understood what this meant, for the sale and the possession of land was unknown to the blackfellows, and even the eight chiefs of the tribe were unconscious of having made any such bargain. They conducted the strangers to the mia-mias which had been built for their use that night, and then returned to their own fires, counting and sorting their new possessions, dressing up in the blankets and necklaces and testing the edges of the new hatchets which were so far superior to their own stone weapons.

Only the dreamer stood apart with half-closed eyes. Banganoo and Latingata watched him as he swayed to and fro, opening and shutting his fists. His slow voice droned like the humming of a bee "The white man shall come as a wind in the night and the mia-mias will be swept away." He moaned for a few minutes before opening his eyes and turning to the children. But Latingata was looking at her face in a mirror, and with little crows of delight Banganoo was sharpening sticks with the white man's jack-knife.

CHAPTER XVI

NEWS IN UJIJI

[A.D. 1871. Stanley finds Livingstone]

The Arabs called him "Soko," which offended him until he grew used to it, for a *soko* was a small yellow ape, a native of the forests on the western side of the Tanganyika where his own people, the Manyema, lived. He was certainly small, and an agile tree-climber, but he was as brown as most negroes and, although he wrinkled his forehead like a chimpanzee when he was angry, he had fine features and well-made limbs, like all the Manyema, whereas the *sokos* had snub noses and very long arms, which they put behind their heads when they walked upright.

He supposed that the Arabs called him Soko because they had found him hiding in a tree during a slave-raid and when one of them had pulled him down by the leg, he had bitten his captor's finger and spat out the blood just as the *sokos* did when they were caught by the hunters. The other Arabs had laughed and cuffed his woolly head without hurting him, but the injured man had been very rough and, instead of chaining him to the children so that he could move comfortably, had yoked him among the older boys with his neck between two heavy

wooden billets. And of course, as the others
were taller, the yoke was too high and he had
been obliged to walk on tip-toe with a stretched
neck, until someone shouted "A dead soko,
oh my uncle, is worth nothing. Put thy little
ape with the children." Then his captor had
unyoked him and chained his ankles instead.
Someone had given him a banana, saying "Try
this finger, oh soko. Thou hast had thy last
taste of human flesh." He had sucked the
banana without speaking. He knew that the
Arab was teasing him slyly, for the Manyema
were cannibals.

But all that had happened when he was a very
little boy. He was ten now and he had been a
slave for two years. The other captives of the
raid had been taken to the coast and sold for
high prices, but he had stayed in Ujiji and
one of the sheikhs of the village had bought
him.

At first he had not been able to do much
because his feet were sore from the chains, but
nobody had minded, and Mohammed ben Saleh,
his master, had plaited a collar of ground lianas
and put it round his neck, fastening him by a
chain to the trunk of a tree, under which he had
plenty of shade and a mat made of bark-cloth
to lie on. When he was well the sheikh's
youngest wife had unfastened the chain, and he
had not tried to run away, because he did not

know how to get back and was afraid of what might happen if he were caught.

He soon learned how to prepare coffee and do little things in the kitchen, but Ujiji was not like his own village. It was restless, for the market was the meeting-place of many tribes who bought cloth from the Arabs, and slave-traders with their human merchandise were continually halting there to feed or to sleep. There was a lack of peace in the very arrangement of the houses, which were set higgledy-piggledy round the market square, instead of standing in a line along broad streets as they did in the Manyema settlements. When Soko was tired of the noise and movement, he thought longingly of his own village, which was surrounded by a hedge of maize, and of the gardens and plantations where the hibiscus fences grew eighteen feet high. The houses in Ujiji were not very different. They had the same clay walls and the leaf stalks of palm split in two to make rafters, and the same thatch of dried banana fronds. But the raised mud verandas of the most important dwellings overlooked the market-place so that there was no privacy.

Soko spent much of his time on the veranda. It was here that he brought coffee when the sheikh was entertaining his friends; and here he stood all the hot afternoon with a horsehair whisk or a palm leaf to keep off the flies and

mosquitoes, while his master smoked a hubble-
bubble and dozed with his white-turbaned head
nodding.

He liked Mohammed ben Saleh. The sheikh
was a gentle master if his slaves served him
well, and he allowed little Soko to play in the
village with the other boys when his work was
finished, encouraging him to bring back the
gossip of the market-place and laughing at the
mixture of languages which he employed, for
he was fast forgetting the corrupt Bantu of his
own people and mingled the many tribal dia-
lects, which he heard round the stalls, with the
Arabic spoken in his master's house.

The manner in which his stories were ap-
plauded was very gratifying to the little slave.
There was always some sort of news in the
village and as he grew older and more accustomed to the languages, he not only gleaned
information but rapidly became an expert at
invention. This enhanced his popularity in the
kitchen, but after a time was coldly received on
the veranda. And once when the market was
unproductive and he had related a more than
usually original piece of news, the mild Mohammed ben Saleh had suddenly seized him by
the elbows, threatening to cut off his ears if he
did not listen more carefully and his tongue if
he could not tell the truth. Soko had struggled
and squealed, swearing with more accuracy

than he knew that there was no truth in Ujiji.
Mohammed ben Saleh laughed and let him go,
but the incident had alarmed Soko, who was
now almost afraid to report any unusual news,
even though he heard it from several different
sources.

One day he stood on the veranda, plaiting the
edge of his loin-cloth between finger and thumb,
waiting for permission to speak. His small
brown body was glistening with perspiration
and the whites of his eyes were very large and
round. He had some news, real news, which
was so exciting that it needed no exaggeration.
Soko was longing to tell it, but he was nervous
lest his master should disbelieve him and cut off
his ears and his tongue before he had time to
prove that it was true.

The sheikh opened a sleepy eye which
twinkled encouragement at the little slave.

"The great master is coming, oh sheikh,"
stammered Soko. "I have seen his servants
Chumah and Susi."

He backed with his hands to his ears, but
Mohammed ben Saleh scarcely looked at him.
He rose as hastily as his vast bulk would allow
and, lifting both hands to the sky, murmured
"Allah be praised," and hurried towards the
market-place.

Soko strolled into the kitchen. He felt important and extremely pleased with himself, but

he had no intention of telling his story without a bribe from the cook, so he leant against the wall, occasionally squashing a bug with his finger and casually dropping hints about surprises and wonderful doings. When the others

Susi

were agog with excitement, he asked for a sweetmeat, which he ate with such silent deliberation that the two slaves who had seated themselves cross-legged before him began to sigh and groan, "Wallah! Oh Soko, bestir thyself." "Tell thy tale, oh my eyes. Hurry, hurry," and they rocked to and fro like Mohammed ben Saleh when he recited the Koran.

Soko wiped his mouth with the back of his hand and his hand with his loin-cloth. "Chumah and Susi are here," he said. "I saw them."

He paused to watch the effect of his statement, which was everything that could be desired. Each slave sat back on his heels, chattering and grinning. They both knew Chumah and Susi, the "great master's" servants. They knew the "great master" too. He was the first white man who had ever been seen in that part of Africa. He had grey hair on his face, and all his servants wore clothes and worshipped in the same odd way as the white man. And they were free, for the great master would not have slaves and even tried to stop the raids. He had a strange way of living, too, as strange as his unpronounceable name, Dr Livingstone. He had been away from his own country for many years and was for ever making lengthy and tedious journeys, seeking for lakes and rivers. He had come to Ujiji a long while ago, but instead of staying quietly in his house, he had disappeared across the Tanganyika and had been gone for two years.

Soko nodded sagely. He knew that the great master had been wandering among the Manyema. He had seen him just before the slave raid and had trotted behind the servants who carried the tents and stores. So unusual an event was firmly printed on his memory, and that was how he had recognised Susi and Chumah in the market-place of Ujiji.

He sucked his sticky fingers and, staring, round-eyed, at his fellow-servants, began an elaborately untrue story of the great master's visit to his father's house, which proved so entertaining that the preparation of supper was forgotten and the temper of Mohammed ben Saleh's wives changed the scene of merriment to one of mourning.

Soko, however, soon forgot his troubles and went about his tasks with a happy grin. His stories of Livingstone and the Manyema gave him prestige in the kitchen, and before long he gained importance in his own eyes, for when the great master arrived in Ujiji, Mohammed ben Saleh often sent the little slave with presents and messages.

Indeed, Soko spent as much time in Livingstone's house as he did in Mohammed ben Saleh's, and he rapidly made friends with everyone, including the youngest inmate which was introduced as "Your little brother from the Manyema" and proved to be a tame *soko*. Many a time the little slave took the ape for a walk, and they could be seen solemnly pacing the veranda, hand in hand, or basking in the sun and playfully boxing one another's ears. If the boy were too rough, the ape took refuge with Livingstone, leaning against its master's knees and hitting its namesake with the backs of its hands. The little creature's antics brought a smile to Livingstone's tired face, and then Soko would joyfully run to the kitchen, crying "The great master's laughing!"

When Susi and Chumah heard this, their black faces beamed with pleasure, and Halimah, the cook, chuckled till her fat sides shook like jellybags. They were all devoted to their master and were overjoyed when Soko's games with the ape amused him. He laughed so seldom that their faithful hearts were troubled about him. Halimah cooked him the best native dishes, devoting endless attention to her task, but he was so weak and ill that he could scarcely eat. He was worried, too, for he had returned to find that all his stores had disappeared in his absence. The great bales of cloth, the coils of wire and the bags of glass beads which were used as money on his journeys and in the market of Ujiji had been stolen by the man to whom they had been entrusted, and Livingstone was without resources.

Soko had often seen gay cloth and beads in Ujiji and wondered how the merchants had come by them. He knew now. They had been sold to make a thief rich, and the great master would have to wait for many a long day before he could make another journey or buy what he needed for his house and his servants.

Soko thought that it would be pleasant for him to rest in Ujiji and could not understand why he was so sad. He consulted Chumah and Susi, but they shrugged their shoulders and rolled their eyes, saying that the great master had set his heart on finding the source of a river and could go no farther until he had stores. Soko was puzzled, thinking that somewhere there must be other white men who would send their brother what he wanted. But Chumah and Susi shook their black heads. The great master had had no letters and no messages for a long, long time. His friends had forgotten him. Perhaps they thought that he was dead. The two men pushed out their lower lips and looked very lugubrious while poor little Soko went home greatly depressed. Like all his race he was superstitious, and he was sure that to be thought dead must bring bad luck.

The idea troubled him and every day, when he had served coffee on Mohammed ben Saleh's veranda, he ran to the market-place, hoping that some messenger had brought a bag of letters for the great master, to prove that his friends remembered him. But the messenger did not come and every afternoon, instead of telling a long story, Soko forlornly blew the charcoal for his master's hubble-bubble into glow, and said "There's no news in Ujiji."

He began to lose hope. It no longer amused

him to scamper on to Livingstone's veranda and play with the little ape, for nowadays his antics seldom raised a smile. The great master seemed to grow sadder and weaker every day. Sometimes he was shivering with cold and sometimes burning with fever. Halimah was in despair. Livingstone would eat nothing which she prepared and his lack of funds prevented her from replenishing the larder, so that she scarcely knew where to turn for food. Chumah and Susi began to look like two lost dogs, and Soko was almost afraid of speaking to them, for when they were not silent and melancholy they were cross. Once when Soko sighed and said "There's no news in Ujiji!" they chivvied him out of their kitchen, flicking him with a wet towel, which stung his bare back as badly as it hurt his feelings, so that he sulked for two days and only recovered when he caught an ominous gleam in Mohammed ben Saleh's eye.

There was no news in Ujiji and Soko had not even the heart to invent. He meandered aimlessly about the market-place, listening without interest to gossip which would once have kept him busily chattering for many a day. People began to tease him. "Oh Soko! Oh Slave!" they cried, "is there no news in Ujiji?" They played tricks upon him, sending him from one shop to another, saying "This merchant" or "That merchant has something for thee," and although he grew tired of the joke, he always went in case he might miss some news. He could not help feeling, however, that matters had been carried too far when he was sent to that very sharif who had stolen the great master's goods. The man was ill-tempered. He had just begun to doze when the little boy arrived, saying "The merchants tell me you have something for me, oh Sharif." He jumped to his feet and seizing a bunch of bamboo canes shouted, "I have this for thee."

Being a slave Soko had some acquaintance with the bamboo and ran, squealing from habit rather than fear, but the sound died on his lips. A loud bang followed by a number of sharp cracks sent him climbing up a tree with all the agility of a terrified monkey. The sharif, who had followed, dropped his bamboos and strode forward, grunting with astonishment.

About two hundred paces from the village stood a gigantic negro carrying a flag. Soko had seen the union-jack above Livingstone's house and some of the Arabs had banners which they brought out on feast days, but this was different. It was spangled with stars like the sky on a dark night and it was striped like the backs of the small antelopes in the forests of Manyema. Near the standard bearer two young negroes held guns like those of the great master. They were firing in the air. Behind them a train of fifty negroes carried bundles of every shape and size. There were donkeys, too, and a cart with two wheels, and in the rear stood a boy with another flag. But it was not the flag which astonished Soko. It was not the large tin bath nor the tent-poles and the packing-cases. *He saw a white man.*

Turning a sort of somersault, he tumbled from the tree and ran shouting towards the caravan. Ujiji had suddenly become a-buzz with excitement. Out of the village swarmed Arab and negro, merchant and slave. Women caught up their children and ran shrieking and chattering. Susi passed in his long white shirt and turban and seized Soko by the hand. In the twinkling of an eye, the flicking of the towel was forgotten, and the little boy ran with all his might, panting with the effort of keeping pace with his friend.

They pushed through the shouting crowd of natives and Arabs and halted before the white man. Soko waited with bated breath. His acquaintance with Livingstone had taught him some English words. He saw Susi go up to the stranger and salute.

"Good-morning, Sir!"

The white man stared. "Who the mischief are you?" said he.

A brilliant smile flashed across the black face.

"I am Susi, the servant of Dr Livingstone."

Soko saw the stranger catch his breath. "What!" he asked, "is Dr Livingstone here?" "Sure, sure, sir," nodded Susi. "Why I leave him just now."

The crowd pressed nearer, talking to the members of the caravan and shouting to one another "Bindera Kisungu" (the white man's flag), but Soko pushed his way past everyone and ran back to Ujiji. He had seen Susi take leave of the white man and run towards the great master's house.

It was strange that everything had happened so quickly. The children of Ujiji had already brought out their drums and were beating a tattoo. From door to door shrilled the zaghreet, that piercing cry of welcome with which the Arab women make known their feasts and weddings. Soko could hear it before he reached Livingstone's veranda.

> Aaaah, oh white man who comes to Ujiji,
>   Lu-lu-lu-lu-lueee;
> Aaah, aaah, oh stranger, oh white man,
>   Lu-lu-lu-lu-lueee!

Soko's feet danced through the dust. He saw Susi talking to Livingstone, who looked dazed. The chief Arabs had gathered in front of his house. His red-sleeved waistcoat and grey trousers were in strange contrast to their long white robes and turbans. As the procession approached through an avenue of people, he stood quite still, gazing, and Soko saw a new light in his eyes.

For a minute the newcomer at the head of the caravan hesitated. Then he stepped forward lifting his hat.

"Dr Livingstone, I presume?"

"Yes," said the great master, raising the blue cap with its faded gold band.

The stranger's voice shook. "I thank God, doctor, I have been permitted to see you."

Soko could understand very little of what they said, but he knew that Livingstone was happy. He saw him lead the stranger on to his veranda and sit beside him on the familiar straw mat covered with a goatskin, while Chumah and Susi stood on each side, bowing and smiling, and Halimah kept poking her head out of the cook-house or flying from veranda to kitchen, now shouting with excitement, now weeping at the condition of the larder.

But Halimah need not have been unhappy, for all day long presents were brought to the great master's house. There were eggs and ground-nuts, fruit and stewed goat's flesh in rice, hashed meat cakes and sweet stuff. Mohammed ben Saleh sent Soko with a curried chicken, and the little boy, proud to be the bearer of such a gift on such an occasion, was hot with indignation when even at night a crowd of Arabs, Wajiji, Wanyamwezi, Warundi

"Dr Livingstone, I presume?"

and others filled the square before the veranda, so that he could scarcely find his way to the cook-house.

That night he yawned sleepily when he made Mohammed ben Saleh's coffee. The old man looked at him. "Is it well, oh Soko, little ape?" he asked.

The slave's stomach contracted and swelled in one immense sigh. "It is well," he answered.

A white man had found the great master. People could no longer believe that he was dead. At last, there was news in Ujiji.

A NOTE ON BOOKS

The following books have been of great use to the authors, who wish to record their gratitude to those writers, living and dead, from whom they have borrowed quotations and information.

CHAPTER I. THE BRISTOL APPRENTICE

Cabot's voyages in Hakluyt, *Principal Navigations, Voyages, Traffiques and discoveries of the English Nation* (the Everyman's Library edition in eight volumes is convenient).

H. P. Biggar, *The Voyages of the Cabots and of Corte Reals, 1491–1563* (Paris, 1903).

CHAPTER II. THE CHILDHOOD OF MARY QUEEN OF SCOTS

R. S. Rait, *Mary Queen of Scots* (Scottish History from Contemporary Writers, No. II, ed. F. Y. Powell, 1900).

A. H. Millar, *Mary Queen of Scots* (1927).

J. T. Stoddart, *The Girlhood of Mary Queen of Scots* (1908).

CHAPTER III. THE VOYAGE OF THE *BONAVENTURE*

Chancellor's voyages in Hakluyt, *Principal Navigations, Voyages, Traffiques and discoveries of the English Nation.*

CHAPTER IV. YOUR HONOUR'S SLAVE

Ralph Fitch's journey in Hakluyt, *Principal Navigations, Voyages, Traffiques and discoveries of the English Nation.*

John Nisbet, *Burma under British Rule and Before* (1901, 2 vols.).

CHAPTER V. THE EAGLE OF THE NORTH

Alice Stopford Green, *The Making of Ireland and its Undoing* (1908).

Irish History from Contemporary Sources (1509–1610), ed. Constantia Maxwell (1923).

Lughaiah O'Clery. *Life of Hugh Roe O'Donnell*, trans. Rev. Denis Murphy, S.J. (Dublin, 1893).

CHAPTER VI. POCOHONTAS, THE LITTLE TOM-
    BOY

Lewis Spence, F.R.A.I., *Myths and Legends of the North
    American Indians* (1914).
H. R. Schoolcraft, *Historical and statistical information re-
    specting the...Indian tribes of the United States* (Phila-
    delphia, 1851–60).
American History told by Contemporaries, ed. A. B. Hart (1901).
E. Keble Chatterton, *Captain John Smith* (Golden Hind series,
    1927).

CHAPTER VII. MARTIN ON THE ISLE OF
    DEVILS

A. E. Verrill, *The Bermuda Islands* (1907).
S. T. Jourdain, *A Discovery of the Barmudas otherwise called the
    Ile of Divils etc.* (privately printed for the Aungervyle Society,
    Edinburgh, 1884).

CHAPTER VIII. NICK AND THE MUTINEERS

Hudson's voyages in Purchas's *Pilgrims*.
T. A. Janvier, *Henry Hudson* (1909).
Llewelyn Powys, *Henry Hudson* (Golden Hind series, 1927).

CHAPTER IX. MEG'S STORY

William Stebbing, *Sir Walter Ralegh* (1891).
Edward Edwards, *Life of Sir Walter Ralegh* (1868).
Martin A. S. Hume, *Sir Walter Ralegh* (Builders of Greater
    Britain series, 1897).
Milton Waldman, *Sir Walter Raleigh* (Golden Hind series,
    1928).

CHAPTER X. FROM CHRIST'S HOSPITAL TO
    SURAT

Beckles Willson, *Ledger and Sword* (1903, 2 vols.).
J. G. Da Cunha, *The Origin of Bombay* (1900).
S. M. Edwards, *The Rise of Bombay* (1902).
E. H. Pearce, *Annals of Christ's Hospital* (1908).
*Christ's Hospital: Recollections of Lamb, Coleridge and Leigh
    Hunt*, ed. R. Brimley Johnson (1902).

CHAPTER XI. THE STRANGE WHITE BIRD

W. Pember Reeves, *The Long White Cloud* (1921).
T. E. Donne, *The Maori Past and Present* (1927).

CHAPTER XII. THE BOSTON TEA PARTY

Harper's Encyclopedia of United States History (vol. 1, Boston).
American History told by Contemporaries, ed. A. B. Hart (1901).

CHAPTER XIII. MURADHANA OF KANDY

M. G. Francis, *A History of Ceylon* (an abridged translation of
Professor Peter Courtenay's work, Mangalore, 1913).
L. E. Blazé, *The Story of Kandy* (Colombo, 1913).
J. P. Lewis, *Ceylon in Early British Times* (Colombo, 1915).

CHAPTER XIV. THE EMIGRANTS' JOURNEY

G. E. Cory, *The Rise of South Africa* (1910–12).

CHAPTER XV. IN THE BLACKFELLOWS' CAMP

A Source Book of Australian History, ed. G. H. Swinburne
(1919).
R. Brough Smyth, *The Aborigines of Victoria* (1878, 2 vols.).
Baldwin Spencer, K.C.M.G., F.R.S., D.Litt., M.A., D.Sc.,
*Guide to the Australian Ethnological Collection exhibited in the
National Museum of Victoria* (Melbourne, 1922).

CHAPTER XVI. NEWS IN UJIJI

H. M. Stanley, *How I found Livingstone* (1874).
*The Last Journal of David Livingstone in Central Africa from
1865 to his death, continued by a narrative of his last moments
and sufferings obtained from his faithful servants Chumah and
Susi*, ed. Horace Waller, F.R.G.S. (1874, 2 vols.).
H. H. Johnston, *Livingstone and the Exploration of Central
Africa* (1912).

Cabot's voyage ....
Somers' " ┴┴┴┴┴┴┴┴┴┴
Hudson Mutineers xxxxxxxxxxxx
Chancellor's voyage +—+—+—+
1ˢᵗ British African Settlers — · · —
Cook's voyage ◆◆◆◆+◆◆◆+◆◆◆◆

Iceland

En
lough
Smills

Pn

Hudson
Bay

Hudson's Strait

C a n a d a

James Bay

North
America

Newfoundland

Cabot Strait

Boston

Chesapeake Bay

James Town

Bermuda

Atlantic
Ocean

R. Bahamas

Pacific Ocean

R. Orinoco

Venezuela

South America

...Bay